How to Design & Build Decks

Created and Designed by the Editorial Staff of Ortho Books

Project Editors
Robert J. Beckstrom
Sally W. Smith

Writers
Mark and Beverly Bremer

Illustrator
Dany Galgani

Ortho Books

Publisher
Robert B. Loperena

Editorial Director
Christine Jordan

Manufacturing Director
Ernie S. Tasaki

Managing Editor
Sally W. Smith

Editor
Robert J. Beckstrom

Prepress Supervisor
Linda M. Bouchard

Editorial Assistants
Joni Christiansen
Sally J. French

Address all inquiries to:
Ortho Books
Box 5006
San Ramon, CA 94583-0906

Copyright © 1995
Monsanto Company
All rights reserved under international and Pan-American copyright conventions.

1	2	3	4	5	6	7	8	9	
95	96	97	98	99	2000				

ISBN 0-89721-261-4
Library of Congress Catalog Card Number 94-69600

THE SOLARIS GROUP
2527 Camino Ramon
San Ramon, CA 94583-0906

Editorial Coordinator
Cass Dempsey

Copyeditor
Barbara Feller-Roth

Proofreader
Alicia K. Eckley

Indexer
Trisha Lamb Feuerstein

Separations by
Color Tech Corp.

Lithographed in the USA by
Banta Company

Architects, Designers, and Builders
Names of architects, designers, and builders are followed by the page numbers on which their work appears.
Archadeck: 20, 21R
Timothy R. Bitts & Assoc.: 6B, 23
Blue Sky Design: 21L
Gordon Builders: 7T
Bowie Gridley Architects: 7T
Gary Cushenberry: 30, back cover TR
Decks by Kiefer: 91
Environmental Creations, Inc.: 9BR
Dan Hasselgrave, Structura: 86
Jeff Hecht, Hecht Construction: 77
John Hemingway: 80–81
John Herbst, Jr., and Associates: 9BL, 84R
Timothy Jones, Calasian Hardscapes: 69
Rick Kiefel: 22B
Christopher Westbrook Klos: 1
Gary Marsh, All Decked Out: 77
McKinney's Custom Deck and Patio: 6T, 7B, 11B
Garry Papers: 22B, 84L
Nancy Pollack and Tom Mossel: 33B, back cover BL
Snow's Garden Center: 34
Eli Sutton with HBM: 22T, 70
Joseph D. Wood, Wood's Shop: 92

Additional Writer
Kathleen Blease

Consultant
Burnie Aarons

Special Thanks to
California Redwood Association
Deborah Cowder
Dean and Denise Fischer
Jim and Caroline Lee
Randy and Carolyn Shane
Smith & Hawken
Melva Storek Interior Design
David Van Ness

Photographic Stylists
JoAnn Masaoka Van Atta: 24–25, 77
Liz Ross: front cover

Photographers
Names of photographers are followed by the page numbers on which their work appears.
Laurie Black: 9T, 11T
Ernest Braun: 1, 6B, 22T, 23, 30, 69, 70, 91, back cover TR
Crandall & Crandall: 9BL, 9BR, 21L, 34, 84R
Stephen Cridland: 22B, 84
Peter Krogh: 7T
Michael Landis: 40-41
Fred Lyon: 4–5
Michael McKinley: 19
Geoffrey Nilsen: 24–25, 26, 33T, 77, 78–79 (all), back cover TL and BR
Robert Perron: 86
Kenneth Rice: front cover
Tom Rider: 80–81
Marvin Sloben: 92
Jessie Walker Associates: 6T, 7B, 11B, 33B, back cover BL

Front Cover
Whether soaring in the trees or stretching out at ground level, a deck brings you closer to nature while giving you all the comforts of home.

Title Page
Every element of this deck, from the change in platform heights to the richness of detail in the decking itself, contributes to the way it blends with the serene setting.

Page 3
Top: Careful planning and coordination, started long before the materials arrive, ensure a successful deck-building experience.

Bottom: A new deck adds living space and makes the most of this attractive waterfront site.

Back Cover
Top left: Wet concrete is pumped into the footing holes for this ground-hugging deck.

Top right: A cascade of steps, benches, deck levels, and planters adds to the visual appeal of this deck while creating flexible, practical spaces for a number of activities.

Bottom left: This cedar deck, left to weather naturally, seems to blend into the surrounding garden.

Bottom right: Plumb, level, and square—checking alignment at the early stages of construction makes the decking and finish work go smoothly.

How to Design & Build Decks

DESIGNING YOUR DECK

The ideal home is a combination of indoor and outdoor living spaces. Most people enjoy spending time outdoors, even when engaged in activities that are usually associated with indoor rooms—activities such as cooking, eating, relaxing, entertaining, working, reading, or pursuing a hobby.

One of the easiest and most convenient ways to create an outdoor living space for pursuing these pleasures is with a deck. It can be anything from a simple platform nestled into a corner of the garden to a multilevel structure attached to the house, its various areas designed for specific functions.

Whatever type of deck you desire, this book will help you design and build it. You will find complete step-by-step guidelines for every stage of the process, from drawing the plans to applying the finish. In addition to the basic techniques for building a simple, durable, and attractive deck, you will find useful design ideas, purchasing advice, maintenance tips, and suggestions for add-ons that will help you create an outdoor living space that is ideal for every member of the household.

Don't let limitations become obstacles. The steep slope, odd shape, difficult access, and limited sun exposure of this site challenged the designer—who turned them into opportunities for creativity.

WHAT INFLUENCES A DECK DESIGN?

Many factors affect the design of a deck, including proposed uses, personal taste, site conditions, regional climate, local building codes, and, of course, cost. During the planning process, you'll consider each of these factors. Take the time to go into each thoroughly, since your deck will be a sizable investment.

Proposed Uses

There are many good reasons for building a deck. Some you may take for granted because they seem so obvious. Others you may not be completely aware of until you start asking yourself, "Why are we building this deck?" It is important to identify and clarify the purpose of the deck as you begin the design, so you can plan the deck to accommodate all of its functions. Prioritizing these functions will help you make compromises and trade-offs when you begin to consider other factors, such as budget, site conditions, and code requirements. Following are the most common reasons for building a deck. Start here to develop and prioritize your own list.

Fun and Enjoyment

The number-one reason for building a deck is to create an area for fun and enjoyment, a space that's inviting, versatile, and attractive. A deck is a fine place for parties and get-togethers. A deck is also an ideal place for getting some sun and spending quiet private time. It is likely that the same deck design can accommodate both needs—public

entertaining and private relaxation—but to be sure, specify what each requires. For instance, entertaining calls for convenient access to the kitchen and bathrooms, an easy transition to other public spaces in the house, enough privacy that neighbors won't be disturbed, and space for tables and chairs. For quiet relaxation, you'll want privacy, intimate sitting areas, convenient access to bedroom areas, serene views, and, if sunbathing is a priority, a sunny exposure.

You may want to use the deck to pursue a favorite activity, such as painting, sculpting, sewing, playing games, reading, playing music, or exercising. An open deck won't be suitable for all of these activities, so you may have to plan such add-ons as protection from the wind, one or two solid walls for sound control, or access to dry storage.

If you're a gardener, you will find the pursuit more enjoyable when all your necessities are close by, so incorporate a storage area on or under the deck for supplies, tools, equipment, and tables. You can even add the garden itself to the deck with a greenhouse or planter.

Each of these decks, just steps from the back door, is designed to provide a place for outdoor fun and enjoyment tailored to the family's interests.

Decks are convenient play areas for children and pets; the interior of your home will benefit while they enjoy the outdoor space. For this use, plan the deck location so you can view activities from the kitchen or family room. Add play equipment, such as a sandbox, playhouse, or play table, plus built-in storage units for toys. Keep the children safe and secure with screening, railings, and lockable gates, and give the pets access via their own special door.

Beautification

A deck can be an elegant addition to a home and the focal point of a yard. If one of the main purposes of your deck is to enhance the architecture of your home or to anchor an overall landscaping plan, you will want to pay special attention to the size, proportions, colors, and details of your deck. You may want to be creative and enhance it with unique touches, such as unusual angles, varying levels, benches, planters, and tables—whatever space allows. Specialty items, such as a pool, pond, waterfall, spa, fountain, and even gazebo, can be incorporated into the overall plan. Even a small deck can add a special accent to your home if the deck is designed well. If you are building the deck to complement the architectural style of your home, you may want to consult with an architect to be sure the deck design is appropriate.

It's possible that the sole purpose of your deck is to convert an unattractive or unusable part of the yard into an attractive landscaping feature. You don't really need the extra living space, but you're looking for a cure for an unsightly lawn, a steep slope, a patch of hard-packed clay, or an awkward transition area between the house and garden. If this is your main reason for building the deck, issues of convenience, access, and usability may not be as important to your plan as the deck's shape, size, and accessories.

Additional Living Space

A deck extends your home's living space at considerably less cost than conventional room additions. A deck will also help reduce the wear and tear on your home's interior. If your purpose for building the deck is to add living space and alleviate crowding in the house, design the deck for specific uses and be sure to include any accessories and special touches those uses require. A deck can take on the intimate character of a family room or den when furnished comfortably, and can be a quiet haven that the entire family can enjoy. Or it can be an auxiliary office—a quiet spot for catching up on personal and business paperwork.

As an outdoor living space, a deck is limited by the local climate. Be realistic about how much you can use a deck, and imaginative about how you can increase the use. As you analyze the site conditions, you may find that an overhead, screens, walls, or other features can double the usefulness of your deck.

Top: This graceful deck, skillfully blended with the architecture of the home, makes the house truly distinctive and memorable.
Bottom: From formal dining to watching the boats go by, this deck serves many purposes.

Site Factors

The site itself plays a large part in the deck design. Factors such as space, access, views, privacy, landscaping features, the architectural style of the home, and, of course, climate all have a significant impact. You are likely to discover conflicts that you must resolve. For instance, the area most convenient to the kitchen may not get any sun (or too much), or the only area large enough for a deck may lack privacy from the street, or the location with the best views may be within the setback area along a property line. Before you try to resolve such issues, however, first look at the site in terms of each of the following factors.

Space

The location and size of the deck will depend on the available usable space. Consider all possible locations for your deck, taking into account property lines, lot-coverage restrictions, setbacks, easements, and current and future landscaping needs that might be affected by them. Identify any area that has enough space for a deck, even if it doesn't seem like the best location at this time. It may turn out to be more satisfactory than you realize at first. Do not overlook areas that seem unattractive or undesirable. They are often the best locations for a deck—the deck not only beautifies the area, it leaves attractive areas intact so they can be enjoyed from the deck.

Access

How the deck is accessed from the house will affect the traffic pattern inside your home. Design wisely. Traffic should flow easily from the deck to the house, particularly to the kitchen and bathrooms. Decide if design elements such as doorways, stairs, railings, walkways, and access for physically challenged persons are needed; these may affect your choice of deck site and how you plan access to it.

An existing doorway usually dictates the placement of an attached deck, but consider installing a new door, if necessary. A large patio door or a pair of French doors offer convenient access for parties and entertaining. If there is already a large window near a potential door location, it may be just the right size to be converted into a door, without requiring extensive structural changes.

A stand-alone deck—one that is not attached to the house—also requires thought about access and its proximity to the house. It must work as a visual and physical transition, not an obstruction, between the house and lawn. Or, if it is several yards from the house, the lawn or a new path must provide the transition.

Consider proximity to the garden as well. Do you want easy access to the garden from the deck? Will a deck in the location you are considering interrupt traffic from one part of the yard to another? Do you want several points of access from the deck, or perhaps a continuous, long step along one or two sides?

Views

There are two kinds of views to consider, and they are equally important: views from inside the house, and views from the deck. First, visualize what you will see from inside your home. Will the deck obscure or enhance the present view? If door and windows are moved, removed, or added, will this dramatically affect what you see from inside?

To consider the views from various potential deck sites, stand on a stool or stepladder at the approximate height of the deck. Observe at different times of the day and, if possible, during different seasons. Note where trees and large shrubs obstruct views. If they are on your property, consider

Identifying Deck Locations

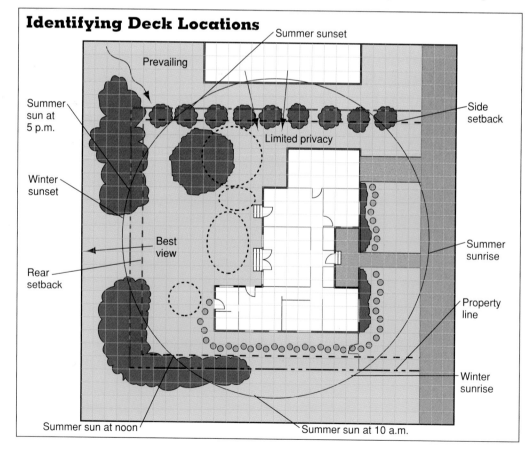

how feasible it would be to have them trimmed or removed; if they belong to neighbors, see if removal or trimming would be acceptable. Make a note of which sites offer the best views, and how you would design the deck to take advantage of those views or to mask less attractive ones.

Privacy

The deck should impart a sense of privacy and enclosure without making you feel cramped and restricted. In other words, you should feel neither on display nor boxed in. Walk around the potential sites and look in all directions, to see if you are in view from neighbors' homes or from the

Top and above: These two decks, positioned to capture sweeping views, still create a feeling of intimacy.

A tall screen provides privacy and helps to define the space.

street. Again, use a stepladder to approximate the deck height. Consider where you may need to erect walls, privacy screens, or fences to make the deck more private, or to retain the neighbors' privacy. Consider noise or other distractions. Will an adjacent empty driveway always be empty? Will sunlight reflected from a large white wall produce an annoying glare?

Natural and Architectural Features

Pay particular attention to natural features that you will want to work into the deck design. These include trees, landscaping, interesting rock formations, attractive retaining walls, and desirable wildlife habitats that may be affected by the deck.

In addition to exploiting some of the natural features of the site, you should also consider the impact of the deck on architectural features of the house, such as doors, windows, rooflines, chimneys, and siding materials. Align the edges of the deck with prominent features, such as corners, and try to balance doors or windows as much as possible. Deck details, such as the finish color or the railing design, can do a lot to harmonize the deck with the architecture of the house.

Don't ignore existing constructed elements in the landscape, such as patios, walkways, and fences. Plan transitions between the deck and these elements to create harmony. For instance, if there is already a patio that you

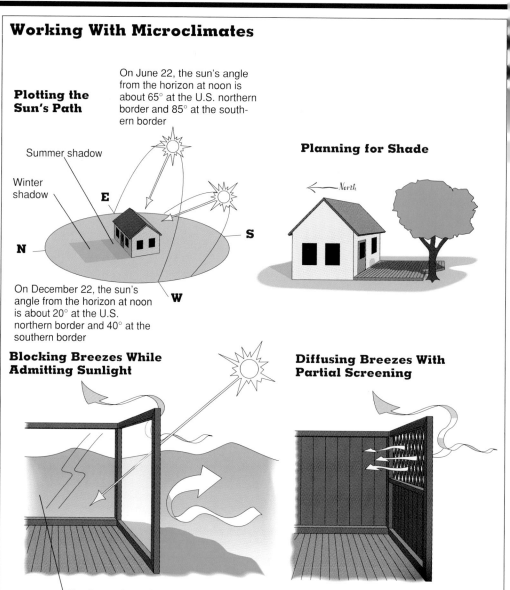

Working With Microclimates

Plotting the Sun's Path

On June 22, the sun's angle from the horizon at noon is about 65° at the U.S. northern border and 85° at the southern border

Summer shadow

Winter shadow

E

N

S

W

On December 22, the sun's angle from the horizon at noon is about 20° at the U.S. northern border and 40° at the southern border

Planning for Shade

North

Blocking Breezes While Admitting Sunlight

Plastic panel or safety glass

Diffusing Breezes With Partial Screening

want to preserve, plan the outlines and proportions of the deck so they align with those of the patio. If you need to remove a patio for drainage or structural reasons (see page 43), you should factor in the cost of doing so when making your final site decision.

Climate and Microclimate

Seasonal weather changes and the effects of varying temperature, sun, rain, snow, ice, and wind must be anticipated. If time permits, keep a journal to establish the patterns of sun position, standing water, and rain and wind direction. Try to recall any unusual weather occurrences. Choose a site that avoids damaging elements,

such as standing water and strong wind, and takes advantage of pleasant conditions, such as cool breezes, shade, and the warming sun.

Note any special soil conditions, such as perpetual dampness or the presence of clay, rocks, and sand. In cold climates, find out the depth of the frost line for your area. These conditions may affect the placement of the footings and posts.

Zoning Laws and Building Codes

Local zoning laws regulate use requirements, lot boundaries, setbacks, utility and right-of-way easements, and the designated use of the land. You will need to consider such laws to find out how close you can build a deck to the property line, how large a deck you can build before the structures on your property exceed a lot-coverage limit, and how high your deck may be if it is not attached to the house. Check with your local planning commission office for information.

Building codes are structural guidelines. They are meant to protect the public from shoddy and unattractive construction. They regulate strength requirements and the types of building materials used. If you're planning electrical or plumbing features, you must also follow local electrical and plumbing codes.

Depending on the size and location of the deck, and the community where you live, you may be required to obtain and post a building permit before construction can begin. Contact your local building department for specific requirements. To obtain the permit, you may be required to submit drawings of the site plan, foundation details, deck components, and elevations.

If you find that the zoning or building codes restrict your ideas for a deck plan too much, you may be able to apply for a variance, which is a one-time-only exemption for a particular construction project.

Also consider unusual conditions that may affect the deck design. In areas where earthquakes, hurricanes, and tornadoes occur, special building codes and construction techniques must be followed carefully. If the house roof is subject to heavy snow loads, make sure the deck won't be in jeopardy from massive snowslides crashing down on it.

Legalities

Before you begin to draw the plans and start building, check the local zoning laws, building codes, and other restrictions that might apply to your location. These laws and regulations ensure that a deck is properly designed and positioned, safe, and well built. Understanding and incorporating the regulations into your deck plans will help the planning (and construction) progress smoothly.

Both of these decks were designed with the sun in mind—one to reach out toward it (top), the other to provide some protective shade.

Other Guidelines

Besides zoning and building codes, your property may be subject to deed restrictions, design review boards, or neighborhood association guidelines. Such guidelines, often called CCRs (covenants, commitments, restrictions), prevent undesirable improvements that could adversely affect other people in the neighborhood. Homeowner associations usually enforce the deed restrictions that regulate size, style, type, building materials, and location. In some instances, these restrictions also establish acceptable noise levels for televisions, music, parties, and other activities.

If you live in an area that has an architectural review board, you may need their permission to build a deck, and be required to present your plans to the group. The board should have written guidelines with requirements and specifications that will help you plan the deck.

Cost Considerations

A major factor in the design of a deck is cost; you want to plan a deck that you can afford. You also want to build a deck that's appropriate for your personal needs, for the length of time you plan to stay in your home, and for your neighborhood. Before you ask yourself how much the deck is going to cost, you should ask yourself how much it should cost—that is, how much can you afford, and how much

of an investment is appropriate for your home and your neighborhood?

How Much Should It Cost?

Establish a budget at the very beginning. Investigate all of your personal financing options and figure out what you are willing to spend. Perhaps you can finance the deck from savings, or you may want to take out a home equity loan. Investigate what funds might be available to you, if any, should you decide to expand the project beyond your budget. The challenge is not to let your eyes get bigger than your wallet.

You should also find out from local real estate agents how much a deck will enhance the value of your home, especially if you are considering a large deck. You may find that the money you spend would be a prudent investment, allowing you to consider a larger budget than you would have otherwise. On the other hand, be wary of overbuilding. If your home is in good condition and is at the lower end of real estate values for your neighborhood, adding a deck would most likely bring a reasonable return on the investment. If your home is already improved more than most others in the neighborhood, adding a deck may yield very little return.

In establishing your budget, don't overlook the pleasure factor. Your home is not just an investment. Consider how much you plan to use the deck and how it will affect the quality of your life, and for

how long. Even if you don't recoup the cost of building the deck when you sell the house, the "lifestyle payoff" could make it one of the best investments you ever make.

How Much Will It Cost?

The final cost of your deck will depend on the size, the materials you choose, structural requirements, the finish details, and the amount of work you will be doing yourself. It is impossible to prepare an accurate cost estimate without a detailed set of plans (see page 26), but you can make some preliminary estimates once you have a general idea of the scope of the project.

One method for rough estimating is to find out how much it cost to build comparable decks in your area. You may have friends or neighbors who have had decks built recently, or you may know a building contractor who has recently completed a deck similar in size and design to yours. Take any numbers with a grain of salt, and be sure you understand whether the cost included all materials and labor, or only portions of one or the other.

Another way to make a quick estimate is with square-footage multiples. The decking itself is easy to figure, because most decking lumber is 2 by 6. You simply double the lineal-foot cost to obtain a square-foot cost. For example, if the lumber is $1 per lineal foot, each square foot of decking

will cost $2. A 16- by 20-foot deck would cover 320 square feet, and the decking would cost $640. For the substructure, footings, stairs, railings, finish, and other features, use the same cost as a residential floor system. Such figures are available from cost-estimating guides, or ask any local contractors you may know. By some inexplicable logic, labor costs in construction tend to be about the same as materials costs, so you can double the materials cost to get a rough total estimate.

Even if you don't have exact figures to work with, you can make a stab at the cost simply by listing all of the deck components and making a reasonable guess as to how much the materials (and labor, if applicable) for each one will cost. Include as many details as you can think of, such as site preparation, alterations to the house, permit fees, and deck finishes (see page 26). Until you have specific plans and can obtain exact price quotes from suppliers and contractors, your estimate will be very rough. It should, however, be close enough for you to see how realistic you have been in your planning; it will also help you prepare a final estimate after you have a set of working plans.

Time, Expertise, and Tools

If you are planning to build the deck yourself, be realistic in assessing your own resources and planning a deck that you can build. Your personal commitment to building

When the Plan Exceeds the Budget

Unless you have planned the Taj Mahal of decks, you'll find that a deck is a relatively spare structure that doesn't seem to offer much opportunity for paring down expenses. Don't despair. Consider the following strategies for reducing costs, before you scrap the project altogether.

• Make sure the estimate is accurate. Do not rely on your own preliminary plans, a designer's estimate, or any contractor's price that is not a firm bid based on the final plans. If you aren't obtaining firm bids, prepare an item-by-item breakdown of all costs, based on prices from as many suppliers as possible.

• Build the deck, as you planned it, in stages. Start with a basic deck. Then, as your budget allows, expand the deck and add more accessories. If the project requires substantial alterations to the house (adding French doors, for instance), postpone them until a later date.

• Reduce the size. Recognize, however, that this cost-cutting strategy has a diminishing point of return: It is very effective if you were planning a large deck, so you can make it substantially smaller, but if the deck was already room-size, you run the risk of making it unusable for your intended purposes. If you can change the purpose of the deck, you can still make a small deck smaller. For instance, if you initially wanted to use the deck for parties or a children's play space, you may have to settle for a balcony-sized deck that serves only for intimate dining or personal relaxation.

• Use less expensive materials. Use pressure-treated construction grade lumber for the substructure. Use more expensive lumber, such as redwood, cedar, or cypress, only for the decking, trim, and railings; or use economy grades of lumber for these components and stain them. Just be sure that the decking and railing lumber is graded for construction use.

• Redesign the railings. If the railings have an elaborate design that uses a large quantity of clear (expensive) lumber, simplify the design and use less expensive sizes, grades, or species.

• Redesign the deck. Lower it far enough that railings won't be required. Change the shape to avoid waste or awkward angles. Detach it from the house if you can then avoid altering doors or windows. Tie the deck into an existing patio or lawn area to expand its usefulness.

• Shop for deals. For decking, search out a recycled-lumber dealer, or a homeowner who is replacing or removing a deck. Buy direct from a mill. Look for neighbors or friends who are also building decks, and buy your materials together to take advantage of quantity price breaks.

• Eliminate or postpone the extras. Can you do without built-in tables and benches, storage cabinets, a lighting system, or a spa? If you plan to install such things later, you should rough in any necessary plumbing, wiring, or structural supports at the time of construction; you can still save by postponing the actual installation.

• Plan to do more of the work yourself. If you have the basic skills and are able to work but didn't want to take the time, you could set aside a few weekends and take on the entire project yourself. This might also be the time to call in some favors.

Begin writing a schedule by estimating the completion date. Take into account existing commitments, such as your job and family obligations. Remember that the seasons determine the number of daylight hours available for working. Of course, temperature, rain, snow, and other weather factors have to be considered. Since most decks are weekend projects, plan to procure materials during the week if possible, so you won't waste valuable work time on the weekends.

Considering Your Expertise

Building a deck requires basic carpentry skills, proper planning, a good set of plans, and a desire to do the work. Avoid tasks that are beyond your abilities. Whether it's designing, handling tools, or exercising physical strength, be realistic and get help when you need it.

Tools

Go through your plans and for each task list what tools you will need. Most of them are probably already in your workshop or can be borrowed from a friend. For one-time use, rent specialty tools, such as posthole diggers, power saws, nailers, power screwdrivers, and motorized concrete mixers. Whenever you rent a tool, be sure you understand thoroughly how to use it, and pay close attention to tool warnings and other safety information.

the deck depends on two variables that can also influence the design—the amount of time you can dedicate to the project and your knowledge of construction. You also need to consider the availability of the tools and equipment you will need for doing the work.

Considering Your Time

Even if you have the know-how to build a complex deck, the project might still be too demanding if you don't have enough time to dedicate to it. Regardless of the design, building projects always take longer than expected, so try to establish a realistic schedule for yourself and your helpers. You should allow time for unforeseen problems and delays caused by the unavailability of materials, unfamiliarity with design and construction, and the weather.

DEVELOPING THE DESIGN

Once you have decided on the site, identified the functional requirements, and chosen the appropriate style for your deck, you are ready to put it all together in a finalized design and draw up a set of plans. The process may go very quickly, or it may take several weeks of revising and refining your ideas.

What Makes a Good Design?

By this time you've probably been considering dozens of design issues and may feel a bit overwhelmed. It's a good time to back up and review a few basic principles.

A good design strikes a balance among several factors: the functional requirements of the deck—all of the uses for which the deck is intended, such as entertaining, relaxing, or gardening; the assets and limitations of the site; the structural requirements of the deck; and special touches that give the deck a sense of style. As you work on your design, you should review the construction guidelines in the third chapter of this book.

The final design must establish the exact location of the deck, define the overall shape and dimensions, detail the structural system, incorporate any stairs or railings into the deck, add whatever accessories may be necessary or desirable, and specify details such as trim, finishes, and color.

There should be a smooth transition from the house to the deck and into the yard or landscape. The deck should not overpower the space, and even though it is an addition,

it should match or complement the existing style and decor of your home.

Expert knowledge of building materials and construction techniques is not required for designing a deck, but you should research, read, and seek advice from knowledgeable sources. Books, videotapes, magazines, and home-improvement stores are excellent sources of specific information. Think through the project and put your ideas on paper. Designing a deck can be an enjoyable task; it's your opportunity to be creative. If this is your first construction project, before you firm up your plans you may want to consult with an architect or a general contractor experienced in deck construction.

Drawing the Plans

A clear, concise, and detailed set of plans is invaluable for ordering supplies, scheduling the work, and keeping the construction steps in proper sequence. Plans also give you the opportunity to adjust the design to fit your budget, schedule, and available materials well before construction begins. After all, it is much easier and less costly to make

adjustments on paper rather than on the deck itself.

The process of drawing the plans will also help you break down large tasks into smaller, more manageable ones. This puts the entire project in perspective by showing what each phase entails. With this information, you can choose which tasks you can do yourself and which will require a professional.

You don't need expensive drafting tools to create accurate, easy-to-follow plans. Just a few basic items will do. Begin with a flat, smooth writing surface, such as a large table or sheet of smooth plywood or similar material. A set of basic drawing tools includes a ruler, a compass, and squares and triangles of various sizes. An architect's scale, also called a three-sided ruler, is invaluable for figuring proportions and scaling drawings. Graph paper is useful and recommended for scaled drawings. Use a soft lead pencil so errors can be erased easily. All these items should be available at local hobby or art supply stores.

Make several copies of the drawings—one or two for yourself, one for your local building department to review before issuing a permit, and, if you are hiring professionals, one for each contractor you ask to submit a bid.

Take a copy of the drawings with you when buying materials. Suppliers are usually willing to help you check or figure the quantities you need.

Drawings to Include in the Plans

A basic set of plans includes all or most of the following drawings. Some of the views, or details, may be combined into one drawing. Check with your local building department to see which ones are required for a permit.

A *site plan* shows the deck's position in relation to the house and yard. Always indicate the direction north, for easy identification.

Elevation drawings show the deck from each side, as if you are standing directly in front of, and level with, the side being viewed.

The *general layout drawing* is an overhead view that shows the decking pattern, plus the location of any built-in or portable extras. You can include present or future landscaping on this layout, or draw a separate landscape layout. When adding trees, be sure to consider their future growth.

Foundation and pier drawings indicate the position of the posts. This helps to eliminate the possibility of forgetting to compensate for the ledger board when measuring for post location.

The *substructure*, or *framing, plan* shows placement and construction details for the ledger board, posts, beams, joists, and bracing. The framing plan and foundation and pier drawings are often combined.

Detail drawings for railings, stairs, built-ins, and other extras should be drawn separately and include the methods of attachment.

Sample Deck Plans

General Layout Drawing

Framing and Foundation Plan

Site Plan

Elevation

Railing Detail

Stair Detail

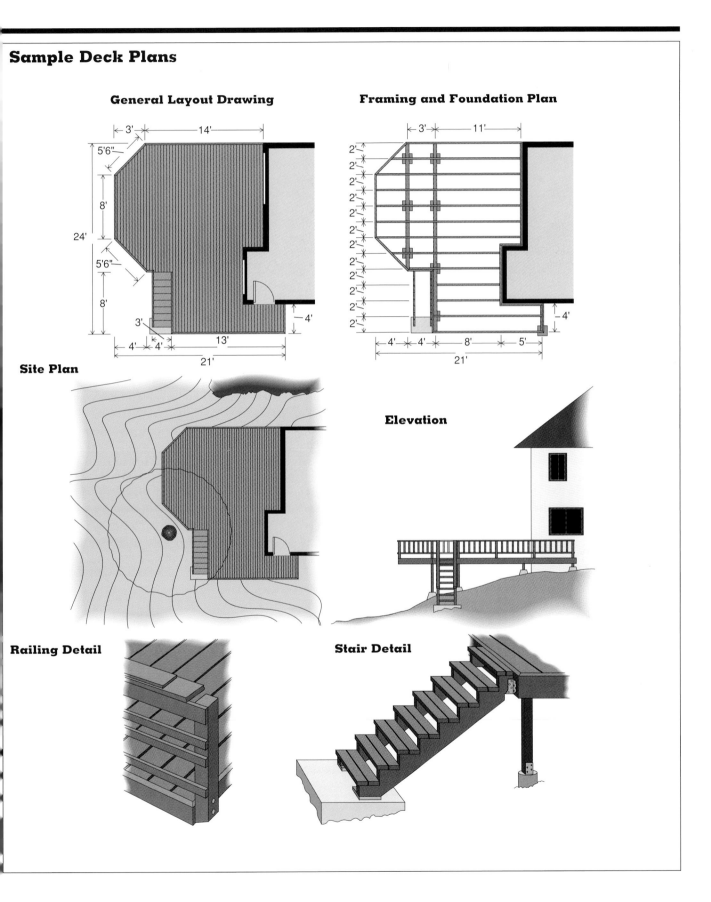

Basic Deck Dimensions

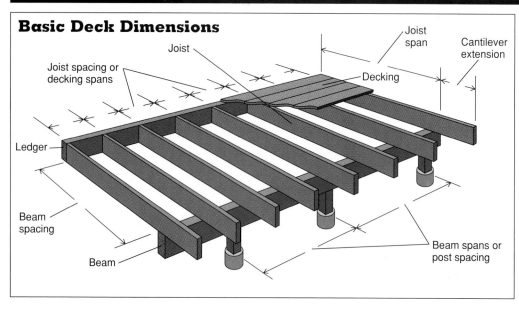

Table 1: Nominal and Actual Dimensions of Lumber

Nominal Size	Actual Size*
1 × 2"	¾ × 1½"
1 × 3"	¾ × 2½"
1 × 4"	¾ × 3½"
1 × 6"	¾ × 5½"
1 × 8"	¾ × 7¼"
1 × 10"	¾ × 9¼"
1 × 12"	¾ × 11¼"
⁵⁄₄ × 6"	1¼ × 5½"
2 × 2"	1½ × 1½"
2 × 3"	1½ × 2½"
2 × 4"	1½ × 3½"
2 × 6"	1½ × 5½"
2 × 8"	1½ × 7¼"
2 × 10"	1½ × 9¼"
2 × 12"	1½ × 11¼"
4 × 4"	3½ × 3½"
4 × 6"	3½ × 5½"
4 × 8"	3½ × 7¼"
4 × 10"	3½ × 9¼"
4 × 12"	3½ × 11¼"
6 × 6"	5½ × 5½"
6 × 8"	5½ × 7¼"
8 × 8"	7¼ × 7¼"

*Dimensions may vary. Always measure.

If future deck additions or accessories are planned, include them in your initial plans. For instance, if a spa or other extremely heavy built-in is to be added later, include the necessary structural elements with the plans now, so you will have the details for roughing in the plumbing and electrical features during construction.

Designing the Structural System

The structural requirements for most decks can be calculated using tables based on typical building code requirements. These requirements are designed to ensure the deck's structural integrity, and they greatly influence a deck's design and construction. If you have special conditions to consider, such as heavy snow loads, earthquake bracing for a high deck, or wind loads, consult with your local building department or a design professional experienced in deck planning.

Once you have established the overall shape and dimensions of the deck, you can work backward in planning a framing system. Start with the decking, which usually runs parallel with the house. Then plan the joist layout by determining the size and spacing of the joists, based on the distance they must span. Then plan the ledger and beam (or beams) that will support the joists. Finally, plan the posts and footings for supporting the beams.

As you plan the deck structure, you may need to revise the size, spacing, or spans of certain members. This is normal. For instance, you may choose a joist size that requires the beam and posts to be located where it will be difficult to excavate for footings, such as directly over a buried pipe. By changing the joists to a larger size, or placing them closer together, you may be able to move the beam out far enough to avoid the obstruction. The size and number of structural members are based on the capacity of the lumber for spanning certain distances and carrying certain loads. You could calculate each individual board based on standard load formulas, but the accompanying tables give you a quicker way to figure minimum lumber sizes and maximum spacings and spans of the deck members. Keep in mind that these recommendations are minimums; you can always choose larger sizes of lumber to increase the strength and stability of the deck. Be sure to check the local building code for any other requirements that may apply.

Follow these steps to plan the deck structure.

Step 1: Be Aware of Actual Lumber Sizes

First, you need to understand how lumber is sized, or dimensioned. Two terms are used to indicate size: *nominal* and *actual*. You'll find that most lumber charts use nominal sizes.

Nominal size refers to the dimensions of lumber before it is kiln- or air-dried and planed, or "dressed." *Actual size* refers to the dimensions after drying and planing. Table 1 shows the difference between nominal and actual sizes.

Here are examples of why it is critical to be aware of the actual size of lumber.

Example 1: In order to save money, or because not enough 4 by 4 posts are available, you decide to fasten two 2 by 4s

Table 2: Strength Groupings of Common Softwoods*

Group A	Cypress, Douglas fir, West Coast hemlock, western larch, southern yellow pine
Group B	Western red cedar, white fir, eastern hemlock, lodgepole pine, Norway pine, Ponderosa pine, sugar pine, northern white pine, redwood (clear, all heart), eastern spruce, Sitka spruce
Group C	Northern white cedar, southern white cedar, balsam fir, redwood (construction heart or better)

*Assumes #2 grade or better.

Table 3: Recommended Maximum Spans for Decking Boards*

	Species Group		
	A	B	C
Laid Flat			
Nominal 1" boards	16"	14"	12"
¾" pressure-treated boards	24"	16"	—
Nominal 2 × 3	28"	24"	20"
Nominal 2 × 4	32"	28"	20"
Nominal 2 × 6	42"	36"	28"
Laid on Edge			
2 × 3	48"	40"	32"
2 × 4	72"	60"	48"

*Spans are based on the use of construction grade lumber or better (select structural, appearance, #1, or #2).
**These spans are based on the assumption that more than one floorboard carries normal loads. If concentrated loads are a rule, reduce spans accordingly.

Table 4: Maximum Joist Spans (beam spacing)*

Joist Size	Species Group		
	A	B	C
12" Joist Spacing			
2 × 6	10'6"	10'0"	9'0"
2 × 8	14'0"	12'6"	11'0"
2 × 10	17'6"	15'8"	13'10"
2 × 12	21'0"	19'4"	17'6"
16" Joist Spacing			
2 × 6	9'7"	8'6"	7'7"
2 × 8	12'6"	11'0"	10'0"
2 × 10	16'2"	14'4"	13'0"
2 × 12	19'0"	18'6"	16'0"
24" Joist Spacing			
2 × 6	8'6"	7'4"	6'8"
2 × 8	11'2"	9'9"	8'7"
2 × 10	14'0"	12'6"	11'0"
2 × 12	16'6"	16'0"	13'6"
32" Joist Spacing			
2 × 6	7'6"	6'9"	6'0"
2 × 8	10'0"	9'1"	8'2"
2 × 10	12'10"	11'8"	10'8"
2 × 12	14'6"	14'0"	12'6"

*Joists are on edge. Spans are center-to-center distances between beams or ledger and beam. Loads are based on 40 psf deck live load plus 10 psf dead load. Assumes a grade equivalent to #2 or better (#2 medium-grain southern pine).

Step 2: Consider Variations in Softwood Strength

Each species of wood has its own level of strength. Softwoods are categorized in one of three groups. *Group A* has the highest strength rating, *Group B* has a middle strength rating, and *Group C* has the lowest strength rating. If you change to lumber with a lower strength rating after the plans are completed, you must refigure spans and sizes. Table 2 shows the strengths of some common softwoods.

Step 3: Establish the Decking Board Sizes and Spans

The decking attaches to the joists to form the surface on which you walk; decking boards transfer the load to the joists. The thickness of the decking boards determines how far they can span; this distance becomes the maximum joist spacing, no matter what size joists are used.

Table 3 shows how close together the joists should be, depending on the species of wood used for the decking boards. The stronger the board, the wider the joist span

face-to-face. Table 1 shows why this will not do.

A nominal 4 by 4 has actual dimensions of 3½ inches by 3½ inches. A nominal 2 by 4 has actual dimensions of 1½ inches by 3½ inches. Two nominal 2 by 4s fastened face-to-face, then, will be 3½ inches wide at one face of the post, but only 3 inches wide on the side. These dimensions would drastically affect the strength and load-bearing capacity of the deck.

Example 2: Let's say your decking plans call for twenty 2 by 12s placed edge to edge. When you get to the lumberyard, there are only fifteen 2 by 12s, so you decide to get ten 2 by 6s to make up the difference. Referring to the chart, you can see that this won't work. A nominal 2 by 12 actually measures 11¼ inches across. Twenty planks placed edge to edge equal 225 inches. However, if you combine fifteen 2 by 12s and ten 2 by 6s, the total is only 223¾ inches— about 1¼ inches shorter than necessary to cover the deck.

can be. Exceeding the spans is not recommended, or permitted by code. To use Table 3, simply match up the species group with the nominal thickness of the decking. For example, nominal 2 by 6 planks laid flat, using wood species Group B, would have a maximum span between joists of 36 inches, on center. Note that with the weaker wood species, using the maximum figures in the table can create an unwanted springy effect. In such cases, position the joists closer together to give the decking a more solid feel.

Step 4: Determine the Joist Sizes and Spans

Once you have figured how far apart the joists can be, based on the species of wood you will use for the decking, consult Table 4 to figure their maximum span—that is, how far apart the beams can be laid—according to their dimension and species. The joist span is measured on center, with the joist installed on edge. For example, using nominal 2 by 6 lumber for joists, in wood species Group B, with 24-inch joist spacing, the maximum joist span, or beam spacing, would be 7 feet, 4 inches.

Step 5: Determine the Beam Sizes and Spans

One or more beams, along with the ledger, support the joists. The size of each beam is determined by balancing two variables: the joist span (the distance between beams, or ledger and beam) and the distance between the posts that support the beam. Generally, it is best to make the beams as large as possible to reduce the number of posts and footings. The posts and footings, however, must not be so far apart that each one bears a load greater than the bearing capacity of the soil itself (for most soils, it's 2,000 pounds per square foot).

To calculate the minimum number of footings and posts required to support the deck: (1) calculate the deck area in square feet by multiplying length by width; (2) multiply one half of the span between the beam and ledger times the length of the deck; (3) subtract this figure from the total deck area; (4) multiply the remaining area of the deck by 50 pounds per square foot (the load); (5) divide the total load by the bearing capacity of the soil (assume 2,000 pounds per square foot). The answer is the number of footings required, if each one covers 1 square foot. For example, a deck measuring 16 feet by 20 feet would have a total area of 320 square feet. If the distance between the ledger and beam is 12 feet, the area of the deck supported by the ledger would be one half of that span (6 feet) multiplied by the length of the deck (20 feet), or 120 square feet. The beam, then, would be supporting 200 square feet (320 minus 120). At 50 pounds per square foot, the load on the beam would be 10,000 pounds. Assuming that the soil could bear 2,000 pounds per square foot, the beam would require five footings

Table 5: Maximum Beam Spans (post spacings) for Decks*

Species Group	Beam Size	\[Beam Spacing (Joist Span), in Feet\] 4	5	6	7	8	9	10	11	12
A	4 × 6	6'	6'	6'						
	3 × 8	8'	8'	7'	6'	6'	6'			
	4 × 8	10'	9'	8'	7'	7'	6'	6'	6'	
	3 × 10	11'	10'	9'	8'	8'	7'	7'	6'	6'
	4 × 10	12'	11'	10'	9'	9'	8'	8'	7'	7'
	3 × 12	12'	11'	10'	9'	9'	8'	8'	8'	
	4 × 12	12'	12'	11'	10'	10'	9'	9'		
	6 × 10	12'	11'	10'	10'	9'	9'	9'		
B	4 × 6	6'	6'							
	3 × 8	7'	7'	6'	6'					
	4 × 8	9'	8'	7'	7'	6'				
	3 × 10	10'	9'	8'	7'	7'	6'	6'	6'	6'
	4 × 10	11'	10'	9'	8'	8'	7'	7'	7'	6'
	3 × 12	12'	11'	10'	9'	8'	8'	7'	7'	7'
	4 × 12	12'	11'	10'	10'	9'	9'	8'	8'	
	6 × 10	12'	11'	10'	10'	9'	9'	9'		
C	4 × 6	6'								
	3 × 8	7'	6'							
	4 × 8	8'	7'	6'	6'					
	3 × 10	9'	8'	7'	6'	6'	6'	6'		
	4 × 10	10'	9'	8'	8'	7'	7'	6'		6'
	3 × 12	11'	10'	9'	8'	7'	7'	7'	6'	6'
	4 × 12	12'	11'	10'	9'	9'	8'	8'	7'	7'
	6 × 10	12'	11'	10'	9'	9'	8'	8'	8'	

*Beams are on edge. Spans are center-to-center distances between posts or supports. Loads based on 40 psf deck live load plus 10 psf dead load. Assumes a grade equivalent to #2 or better (#2 medium-grain southern pine).

Table 6: Maximum Post Heights for Decks*

Load Area (Beam Spacing × Post Spacing) in Square Feet

Species Group	Post Size	36	48	60	72	84	96	108	120	132	144
A	4 × 4	Up to 12' high				Up to 10' high		Up to 8' high			
	4 × 6	Up to 12' high								Up to 10' high	
	6 × 6	Up to 12' high									
B	4 × 4	Up to 12' high		Up to 10' high			Up to 8' high				
	4 × 6	Up to 12' high				Up to 10' high					
	6 × 6	Up to 12' high									
C	4 × 4	To 12'	Up to 10' high		Up to 8' high			Up to 6' high			
	4 × 6	Up to 12' high		Up to 10' high			Up to 8' high				
	6 × 6	Up to 12' high									

*Loads based on 40 psf deck live load plus 10 psf dead load. Grade is #2 and better for 4 × 4 posts and #1 and better for larger sizes. Group A: Douglas fir (north), larch, and southern pine. Group B: Hem fir and Douglas fir (south). Group C: Western pine, western cedar, redwood, and spruce.

Example: If the beams are spaced 8'6" OC and the posts are spaced 11'6", then the load area is 98 square feet. Calculate post heights based on next larger area: 108.

if each one were 12 inches square (1 square foot). If the footings were 16 inches square (2 square feet), only three would be required.

Step 6: Determine the Post Sizes and Spacing

The size of the posts is determined by the overall load and the height of the deck. To figure the load, multiply the beam spacing (joist span) by the post spacing (beam span). If the result falls between two numbers on the chart, use the higher of the two.

The structural underpinnings of a deck are an interdependent system based on the variables of spacing, spans, and lumber size.

Basic Stair Dimensions

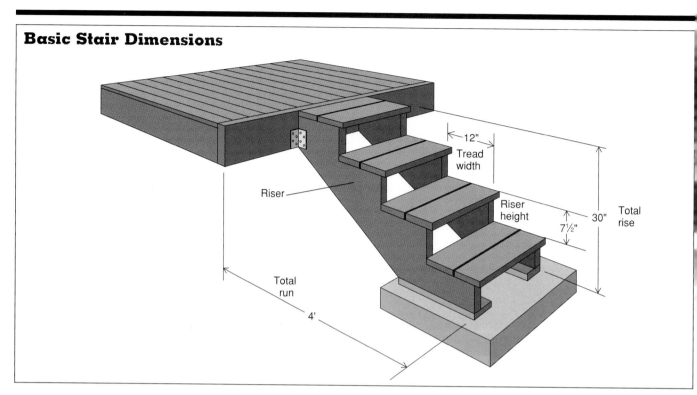

Riser

12"
Tread
width

Riser
height

7½"

30"

Total
rise

Total
run

4'

Riser and Tread Proportions

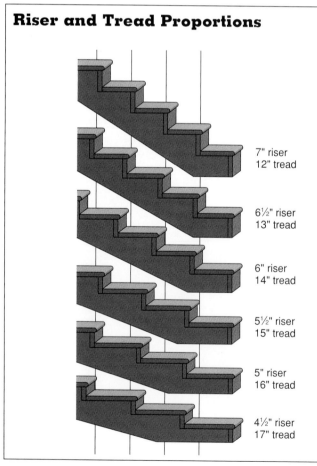

7" riser
12" tread

6½" riser
13" tread

6" riser
14" tread

5½" riser
15" tread

5" riser
16" tread

4½" riser
17" tread

This long stairway has cutout stringers to support the treads and risers.

Planning Stairs and Railings

Although it is best to plan the stairs and railings after you have designed the rest of the deck, do not consider them mere afterthoughts. Railings, especially, can dominate the appearance of a deck. Stairs and railings have very important safety functions, and both have strict code requirements that dictate much of their design.

Stairs

Treads, risers, and stringers are the components of stairs. Risers are optional, provided that the area under the stairs is maintained attractively. Stairs must be strong enough to carry substantial loads. To do this effectively and safely, the treads must have the same dimensions throughout, and the risers should be the same height on all steps.

Check building codes for stair requirements in your area. The stringers are usually made of 2 by 12s. For single steps, the stairs can be made completely from 2 by 6s, using one 2 by 6 for the riser and two 2 by 6s for the tread. Although most codes require that stairs have a maximum riser height and minimum tread width of 7½ inches and 11 inches, respectively, there is no reason why the stairs cannot have less of an incline—a 6-inch riser and 14-inch tread, for instance, or a 5½-inch rise and 15-inch tread. Such dimensions have a more luxurious feeling, conducive to lingering and relaxing. They are also safer.

When the stairs are assembled, the leading edge of the tread should overlap the riser below by ½ inch to create a shadow line, which helps define the steps. The upper ends of the stringers should be attached to the deck header with joist hangers. The lower ends of the stringers can be placed on concrete, bricks, or pressure-treated lumber specified for ground contact. Never rest the lower ends of the stringers on bare ground. It is unstable, and the wood will absorb ground moisture, leading to rot and insect infestation.

An alternative to wood steps is to use prefabricated concrete steps, or build forms and pour concrete ones.

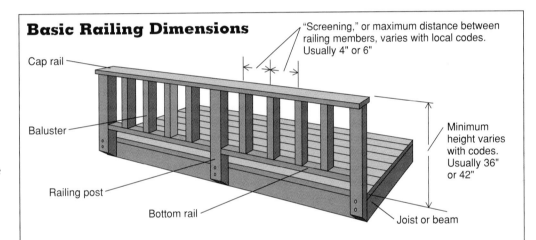

Basic Railing Dimensions

Cap rail

Baluster

Railing post

Bottom rail

"Screening," or maximum distance between railing members, varies with local codes. Usually 4" or 6"

Minimum height varies with codes. Usually 36" or 42"

Joist or beam

When a deck includes several different stairways, even if they are not connected, the riser height of all steps should be exactly the same.

This railing features a sunburst design and beveled post caps.

Altering and Upgrading Decks

If you have an existing deck that is uninteresting yet structurally sound, you can transform it into a more attractive and functional outdoor room.

•Change its size and shape. Increase the surface area with stand-alone or attached additions. For more interest, add angles, curves, or levels.

•Add accessories. Built-ins make the deck more inviting and useful. These can be simple wood planters or an intricate overhead with canvas inserts.

•Correct an ineffective layout. If access to the deck area is a problem, rearrange the traffic pattern, move stairs, and eliminate obstacles on the deck.

•Replace or remove any broken, outdated, or unused accessories.

•Add new landscaping. This is an economical and relatively easy way to give the deck a new look.

Once planned, your deck's transformation can happen all at once, or as your time and budget permit.

Railings aren't just a finishing detail—they can be the most dramatic part of a deck's design.

Another alternative is a ramp for garden carts, wheelchairs, or similar wheeled items.

Railings

All raised decks should be protected by railings for safety as well as appearance. Railings can support flower boxes or be part of a built-in bench system. They can be plain or ornate, open or solid, basic or custom-made.

Many types of materials can be used to fill in the area between the top rail and the deck. The possibilities include redwood lattice, wood spindles, vertical or horizontal wood strips, sheets of clear rigid plastic, wrought iron, rope, cable, or canvas.

Local building codes require railings for stairs when there are a certain number of steps in a set. The railing is typically 30 to 33 inches above the steps. If the deck is elevated, the railing is typically 36 to 42 inches above the deck surface. The railing must be able to resist a horizontal force of at least 15 pounds per lineal foot. For child safety, the maximum distance between railing members is 6 inches for most local codes (4 inches for some).

Adding Special Features

In planning your deck, consider any special touches and custom features that might personalize and enhance the deck's overall look, usefulness, and function.

Types of Additions

Deck add-ons and accessories can be as simple or as elaborate as you desire. Start by listing the various refinements that would suit your needs and complement the planned uses for the deck. Incorporate as many as you can into your original design.

For entertaining and cookouts you might want to include built-in tables and benches, counters for preparing and serving food, a wet bar, and cabinets for cooking accessories. With proper safety considerations, you can incorporate a portable propane grill, hibachi, or built-in barbecue.

Other additions to consider are built-in planters, privacy screens, an overhead for complete or partial shade, and skirts that enclose the area underneath the deck.

As you plan your deck, think about its storage possibilities. Decks are excellent sources of additional storage in many homes. Everything from toys, sporting equipment, garden tools, and lawn furniture to unsightly garbage containers can be stored on, below, or adjacent to the deck. Use privacy screens or built-in storage areas to keep these items organized and out of sight.

Electrical and Plumbing Needs

It is important to consider current and future electrical and plumbing needs on your deck. Include all of them in your deck design even if you are planning to install only some of them initially.

Carefully plan the number and location of electrical outlets, types of general and decorative lighting, and other electrical requirements. Also consider extras such as cable television hookups, telephone jacks, and fans.

Features that require plumbing include a shower, sink, wet bar, spa, and plant watering hookups.

Check and follow local codes when planning electrical and plumbing features.

When to Install Accessories

Incorporate everything into your initial design, but then ask yourself when you want each item installed. With advance planning and a good set of deck plans, many accessories can be planned for now and installed later.

For example, you may want a built-in food preparation area. Include counters, cabinets, and electrical and plumbing needs in your plans. This way, when you're ready to finish this special feature, the space is allotted and access to utilities has already been thought out.

Many additions can be built off-site in your garage or workshop. These are perfect projects when weather prevents working outside or when your time is limited to sporadic evenings or weekends. If you have several deck additions planned, keep on hand the plans and materials for at least one or two.

A spa requires specialized wiring that should be done by a qualified electrician.

PLANNING AHEAD

One fortunate aspect of building a deck is that life in the house is disrupted much less than with other home-improvement projects. However, this does not mean that building a deck is a casual weekend task. It is a serious project. Structurally, a deck has the same requirements as the floor system in your home. Architecturally, it is a major feature of the home's facade and landscape. Its constant exposure to weather requires careful construction techniques. For these reasons, even though you've designed and planned precisely what you want in a deck, you must plan how you are going to build it with the same precision.

In this chapter, you'll learn how to review carefully every phase of the project before it starts. Now is the time to decide which tasks you will want to do yourself and which ones you should leave to a professional. You should also make careful estimates of the materials you'll need, acquire the necessary tools, and adjust and finalize your budget.

Obtaining materials, having them delivered to the job site on time, and rounding up the right tools are some of the important preliminary steps in any deck-building project.

PLANNING FOR SUCCESS

The key to success? Knowing ahead of time what you want to do, then planning how you're going to do it. Estimating costs, obtaining a permit, scheduling construction, and ordering materials are important elements of planning, but your first step should be to define your own role.

Preparing Yourself

First, determine which tasks you'd like to do yourself. Are you physically capable of doing them? Will you want or need help? Determine which tasks require helpers, and find some who are capable, both physically and in terms of attitude. Don't turn your deck construction into a party—this can be dangerous and a serious liability!

Second, assess your construction knowledge. Now is the time for you to do some research. Check the local library, home-improvement centers, and bookstores for informative magazines, pamphlets, videos, and books.

Third, assess your mental preparedness. Are you ready to cope with problems and snags? Are you likely to complete a task, once you have started? Are you asking yourself to do more labor or technical work than you honestly can or should handle? Will you be able to enjoy the process (and help others enjoy it, too)?

The main purpose of this book is to encourage you, and to teach you, to build a deck yourself. However, don't hesitate to hire professionals for any task you don't feel confident doing, or don't have the time or desire to complete. If you plan to hire hourly workers or unlicensed professionals who are not members of your family, be prepared to take on the responsibilities of an employer. These include reporting wages to the IRS, withholding state and federal taxes, and carrying a workers' compensation insurance policy (your homeowner's policy may include coverage; be sure to check).

Verifying Costs

By now, with your deck design completed, you probably have a general idea of how much the deck will cost. Rough estimates, or at least hopeful expectations, go hand in hand with the deck design process. Now it is time to verify those estimates—to find out the exact cost of materials, tools, and equipment, and to get competitive bids for labor or professional services you may need. These costs will be the basis of an itemized budget you can develop for managing your deck project. If you're having a general contractor build the deck, he will make such a list based on your plans and his experience. However, it will still be useful for you to develop your own budget so both of you can clarify exactly what the contractor's bid includes.

First, make an itemized list of all the materials needed to build the deck. Start the list now, while you are reading this book and the information is fresh in your mind. Then modify the list as you develop your design. Divide the list into categories, such as lumber,

This deck, built by the homeowner, reflects careful planning and skillful attention to every detail, such as the hatch for the garden hose visible in the foreground.

Guidelines for Selecting and Working with Contractors

Building the deck yourself can be personally rewarding and, of course, it can save you money. But don't hesitate to hire a contractor to handle aspects of the construction you feel uncomfortable about or may not have the time to do.

The key to finding the right contractor and working effectively with him or her is communication. Understanding the basics of constructing a deck will help you communicate what you want and expect, so the contractor can develop an estimate that meets your exact specifications. It will also help you listen to the contractor's suggestions. Keep in mind that a professional possesses a wealth of knowledge, so listen carefully to whatever he or she has to say. Here are questions to ask and tips for selecting and working with a contractor.

•Get bids from several contractors, and make sure each is bidding on exactly the same specifications. Bids should be detailed and in writing. A carpenter, for example, should include the species, grade, and size of the lumber to be used, and the method of attaching it.

•Ask for and check the references of each contractor. Talk to former customers about their overall satisfaction, the quality of the materials used, and whether the job was completed on schedule. Ask if the contractor was reliable, professional, and easy to work with. Check with the Better Business Bureau in your area for any complaints; if possible, look over recent work each contractor completed.

•Ask to see a license and proof of insurance, to protect yourself from liability in case of an accident.

•Read the contract thoroughly; make sure you understand it, and ask for your own copy. Be sure every detail you discussed with the contractor is included; this protects you. Be sure the contract contains the total cost of the job, method of payment, starting and completion dates, and material specifications. It should say who is to obtain the permit, provide materials, and dispose of trash.

•Get any changes and their costs in writing.

•Request a contractor's affidavit with waivers of mechanic's liens before final payment is made.

•Be prepared when work starts. Provide a place for contractors and workers to park. Clarify responsibilities and liabilities for tool storage and tool security. Deck construction requires little access to indoors, but find out ahead of time how much access will be necessary. Discuss such details as use of the telephone, bathroom, or refrigerator, or household rules about smoking, radios, and pets. Also clarify starting and quitting times.

hardware, concrete, reinforcing steel, deck finishes, tools, and so forth, so you can tailor your list quickly to the type of supplier giving you a price quote (for example, some lumberyards may not carry concrete or hardware). Contact several suppliers before choosing one. And remember, many suppliers offer discounts for large-volume purchases, so try to find suppliers who can bid on your entire materials list. When choosing your materials, keep in mind that common materials are readily available and less expensive than specialty items. Special orders could also cause delays. Be sure to clarify with the supplier whether or not delivery is included. See page 32 for further information about materials.

Next, itemize all the services you will need, such as plans drawing, excavation, concrete pumping, carpentry, tool rental, debris removal, and painting or staining. Again, a general contractor will coordinate and subcontract for these services, but it is useful for you to itemize them so you can clarify who will be responsible for each task when you obtain bids for the job.

After you are sure of all the costs, develop an itemized budget. Use the lists of materials, services, and professional assistance you have created and assign a cost to each item or category of items. There are always extra expenses and hidden costs in any project, so add another 10 percent to your budget to cover them. These

costs, which are mostly incidental, are easy to overlook, but they can add up significantly over the course of a long project. They include:

•Permit fees
•Employer expenses for hiring labor (payroll taxes, workers' compensation insurance)
•Expensive substitutions for materials that are unavailable
•Tools, either purchased or rented
•Sharpening or replacing blades
•Power cords
•Safety equipment: goggles, gloves, dust masks, hard hats
•Vehicle mileage, wear and tear
•Increased use of telephone and utilities
•Debris box rental or dump fees

•Tarps or plastic sheeting to cover supplies
•Replacing siding, plumbing, or wiring "while we're at it"
•Patching the siding around new windows, doors, or steps
•Delivery charges for materials
•Repairing or replacing damaged plants, lawn, sprinklers, walks, fences
•New landscaping around the deck
•New lighting
•New deck furniture
•Photographic film and developing

If the budget exceeds your limit, you can then make adjustments to your design or chosen materials before you begin building. If you try to make changes during the actual construction, you will be more likely to make mistakes and you will probably have to deal with delays.

Scheduling the Project

Make a schedule listing all tasks, from buying materials through finishing touches, in step-by-step sequence.

Then break down each large task into several smaller ones. For example, site layout could include: measure deck area, mark off area with stakes and batter boards, run string off ledger and batter boards. After breaking down the project into small tasks, you may find that you'll want to tackle most of the work yourself. Small tasks make the project seem less overwhelming, and you can slip them in whenever you have only a little time available. Breaking the job down into smaller jobs also helps you purchase the right materials at the right time.

After you list the tasks, indicate an estimate of hours and the anticipated completion date. Allow time for adverse weather, shopping for materials, and inspections (normally, one inspection before the concrete is poured, and a final inspection after the deck is completed). Include time for making alterations to the house, such as door access and other structural changes, and determine if these will be done before or after the deck is built.

Include time in your schedule for deliveries and for work being done by contractors. If

Checklist of Tasks

Use the following list as a guide to create a schedule; rearrange, delete, or add steps according to your plans. To create a master checklist of tasks and costs, you may want to add columns for cost, estimated time for each task, start date, and finish date.

- List design requirements for the deck (such as functions and uses)
- Evaluate site factors
- Investigate legalities, such as zoning regulations, building codes, and permit requirements
- Determine time and experience required

- Draw up a set of working plans
- Prepare a list of materials
- Establish costs and a budget
- Develop a construction schedule
- Select contractor(s)
- Purchase materials and order any specialty items
- Remove existing structures or landscaping, as required
- Make alterations to house
- Set up work site: Organize tools; plan a storage area; plan for storage and removal of debris
- Prepare the deck site

- Attach ledger board
- Build batter boards and lay out post locations
- Dig footing holes
- Pour concrete footings and piers
- Erect posts
- Install beams
- Install joists and joist header
- Install blocking or bridging
- Rough in electrical or plumbing
- Install decking
- Assemble railings
- Build stairs
- Build and add accessories
- Apply finish

you schedule changes, be sure to contact suppliers and contractors as far in advance as possible.

Three Important Details

It's easy to launch into a construction project without taking care of three important details ahead of time: having the right tools; providing an appropriate space to store materials and tools; and planning for debris removal. Although these seem like "bridges to cross when I get there," not being prepared for them can easily disrupt a construction project. More importantly, planning these details ahead of time will keep the construction site clean and organized—and safe.

The Right Tools

Deck building doesn't require a lot of tools, just the right ones. Gather your tools together and review the lists that follow. Most of the tools are inexpensive and easy to find, but you may want to rent or borrow any you don't have.

Site Layout

- Tape measure (1 inch by 25 feet), for general measurement
- Tape measure (100 feet), for laying out large deck site
- Sledgehammer, for driving stakes
- Nylon string (mason's twine), for laying out string lines
- Water level or builder's level, for establishing level marks on the site
- Carpenter's level, for aligning posts vertically and for general leveling
- Torpedo level, for aligning forms, piers, and brackets

- Plumb bob, for laying out site and positioning components

Excavation and Concrete Work

- Shovel (garden spade), for preparing site
- Rake, for preparing site
- Posthole digger or power auger, for digging footing holes
- Shovel (square nose), for squaring hole edges
- Shovel (trenching), for widening footing area at bottom of deep hole
- Wheelbarrow, for moving materials and mixing concrete
- Hacksaw, or metal cutoff blade for circular saw, for cutting reinforcing steel
- Cement mixer or container for mixing concrete, depending on amount of concrete
- Buckets (5 gallon), for measuring concrete ingredients and cleaning tools

Basic Tools for Building a Deck

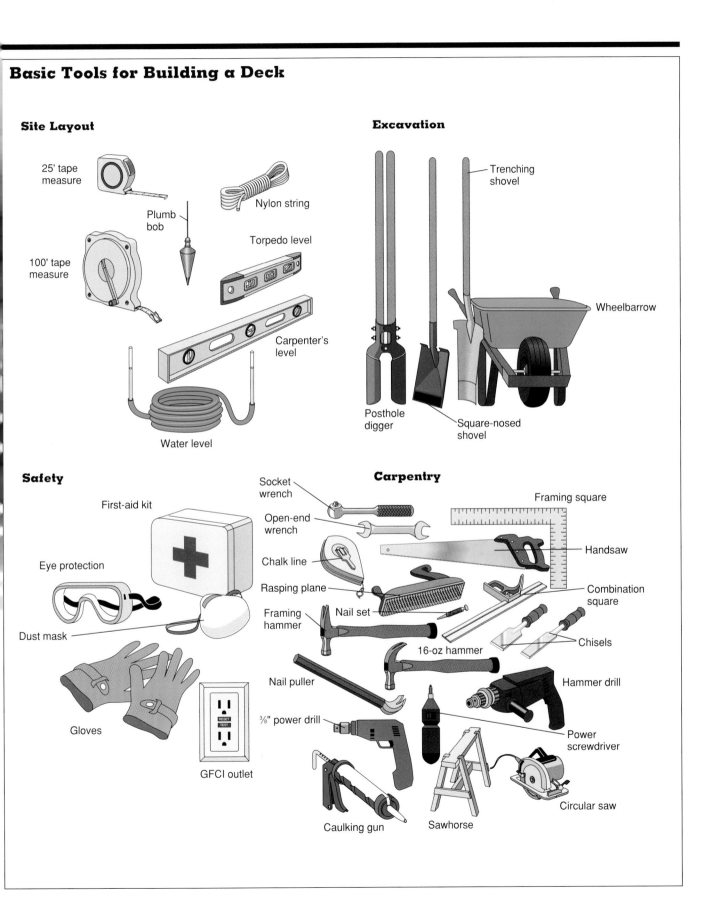

Site Layout

25' tape measure

Plumb bob

Nylon string

Torpedo level

100' tape measure

Carpenter's level

Water level

Excavation

Trenching shovel

Wheelbarrow

Posthole digger

Square-nosed shovel

Safety

First-aid kit

Eye protection

Dust mask

Gloves

GFCI outlet

Carpentry

Socket wrench

Open-end wrench

Chalk line

Rasping plane

Framing hammer

Nail set

Framing square

Handsaw

Combination square

Chisels

16-oz hammer

Nail puller

Hammer drill

⅜" power drill

Power screwdriver

Caulking gun

Sawhorse

Circular saw

Carpentry

- Combination square, for marking crosscuts
- Framing square, for marking crosscuts, squaring corners, and laying out stringers for stairs
- Chalk line, for marking straight lines and for an extra plumb bob
- Handsaw (crosscut) or power circular saw
- Hammer (20 ounce, smooth face), for framing
- Hammer (16 ounce), for finish trim
- Nail puller (cat's-paw) or pry bar
- Nail set ($5/32$ to $1/4$ inch), for driving nail heads below the wood surface
- Chisels ($3/4$ or 1 inch, and $1 1/2$ inch), for notching and prying
- Rasping plane or power sander, for smoothing edges

- Power drill ($3/8$ inch, cordless or conventional), for drilling pilot holes and holes for carriage bolts and other hardware
- Power screwdriver with Phillips head, square-drive, or hexagonal bit, for driving deck screws
- Hammer drill, for drilling into concrete or masonry (if necessary)
- Wrenches (open end, adjustable, or socket), for assembling deck components with lag screws, carriage bolts, or machine bolts
- Caulking gun, for applying caulk and adhesives
- Sawhorses (sturdy), for supporting lumber to be cut
- Brushes, rollers, or garden sprayer, as needed, for applying finish

Safety Equipment

- GFCI-protected outlet, or portable GFCI, for plugging in power tools and extension cords
- Ribbon or rags, for flagging dangerous obstacles, such as steel stakes or low concrete piers that will be left exposed while you're not working
- Eye protection, such as goggles or safety glasses
- Gloves, especially for working with concrete and pressure-treated lumber
- Dust mask
- Hard hat, for anyone working below others
- First-aid kit, with tweezers

Storage

Set up a secure storage space near the job site for lumber, supplies, and tools. It could be a garage, locked shed, or even a secure yard, but it must be easily accessible from the work site. Be sure to store toxic substances, such as stain and adhesives, in a locked cabinet or shed.

The storage site you choose should be high and dry. Cover the materials with plastic sheeting, whether indoors or out, to protect them from dirt and the elements. To keep lumber from warping, be sure to stack it on a perfectly level platform or with stickers (lath or 1 by 2s) between levels. Don't let the lumber sag or lean against a wall, or it may warp permanently. Construction grade lumber can be exposed to the sun, but it still must be stacked properly and off the

ground. Other types of lumber must be stacked inside, covered, or in the shade.

Devise a way to keep nails, screws, bolts, and other hardware organized. Empty paint cans or coffee cans are ideal for nails and screws—label each one clearly.

Don't let supplies and lumber become "ankle busters," left where you can trip over them while you're working. Store and organize them in one area in a way that gives you easy, clear access.

Finally, be sure to line up helpers for deliveries, to assist you in moving materials from the street or driveway to the storage area.

Debris Disposal

Building a deck generates considerable construction debris and trash, and some of it may be toxic. Plan ahead for its disposal. Because of environmental concerns, most locales now have special collection points for unused paints, solvents, preservatives, and other toxic materials. Check the regulations in your area for the substances that require special handling.

If you have scraps and leftover pieces of pressure-treated lumber, do not burn them. Dispose of them as ordinary garbage, or keep a few scraps on hand for blocking, garden projects, or other uses.

If you are left with a large pile of dirt, use it to grade and landscape the area around the deck or fill in low spots in your yard or find someone who needs clean fill, or take it to your landfill.

The redwood in this multilevel deck, which was designed and built by the homeowner, has been finished with a preservative to retain and enhance the original color.

Safety

Any construction site has potential dangers, but you and your helpers can prevent accidents with a little know-how and good judgment. Here are some tips for working with tools and materials and for keeping the work site safe.

•Personal gear. Your eyes are very vulnerable to contact, dust, and chemical injuries. Always wear safety glasses or goggles when using power tools or when performing any task that could put your eyes at risk, such as spraying wood finisher. Also use a dust mask when sawing pressure-treated wood and applying finishes. Unless you are walking on the joists or laying down decking, wear shoes with hard soles that resist nails and other sharp objects.

•Power tools and extension cords. When you use power tools while standing on the ground, you are at risk from electrical shock from a malfunctioning tool or cord. To protect yourself, always plug power tools and extension cords into receptacles that have GFCI (ground fault circuit interrupter) protection. You may already have an outdoor GFCI receptacle; if not, look for one in your bathroom and run a cord from it. Otherwise, buy a portable GFCI outlet; you can plug it into an ordinary electrical receptacle (grounded or ungrounded) and plug cords for power tools into it.

•Heavy loads. Don't lift heavy objects yourself. Always have a helper ready to assist in carrying heavy and bulky materials and in lifting deck components into place. The greatest risk is lifting and twisting at the same time. You may want to wear around your waist a special support belt, available at most home-improvement centers.

•Ladders. Because of the danger of electrical shock, pay attention to overhead power lines when using a ladder. Never stand on the top platform of a stepladder; it is not designed to accommodate loads at its very top. Never climb a ladder higher than a manufacturer recommends, and don't use a ladder with broken parts.

•Work site. Clean up the site regularly. Remove all debris to prevent falls and slips. Don't leave tools and supplies lying where someone can trip over them. Be especially careful about how you handle boards with nails and where you place them; remove protruding nails or bend them over so no one will put a nail through a shoe. Cover footing holes and other excavations with sheets of plywood when you leave the job site. Don't use plastic or tarp for this purpose—they cannot support a person's weight. If the holes are too large for plywood, barricade and fence off the area, and post a "Keep Out" or "No Trespassing" sign.

•Utilities. Contact your local utility to come to the site and mark any underground television cable, power, telephone, water, and sewer lines, as well as gas lines, before you begin any digging, especially close to property lines. In addition, if you have a septic tank and leach field, mark the location before you begin to dig.

•Electrical installations. If you are unfamiliar with electrical wiring, contact a licensed professional to do all installations.

•Pressure-treated lumber. Always wear safety glasses and a dust mask when sawing this lumber. After touching it, wash your hands before eating, drinking, or smoking. Dispose of leftover wood and scraps in regular household trash or according to local requirements. Never burn pressure-treated lumber—it produces toxic fumes.

•Materials and supplies. Some building supplies, such as preservatives, finishes, and adhesives, are toxic. Read and follow the manufacturer's labels for safe use, storage, and disposal.

•Debris. To help protect the environment, follow local regulations or the manufacturer's recommendations when disposing of construction debris, toxic materials, and other trash.

•Tool safety. Use the right tool for the job. Keep blades sharp. Always read the owner's manual and understand the manufacturer's instructions before using any power tools. Never use power tools outdoors when it's raining or let a power cord connection lie on damp or wet ground.

•Clothing. Wear comfortable, loose-fitting garments. Don't wear clothing or jewelry that could get caught on tools or deck components. If you are wearing loose-fitting long sleeves, roll them up so there's no chance they will be caught by power tools. Wear boots or heavy work shoes during excavation and framing to protect your feet from falling objects and boards with protruding nails. You can wear lighter weight shoes, if you prefer, during installation of the decking and railings.

•Helpers. Instruct your helpers about work safety, including procedures for an emergency. Check your homeowner's policy to be sure that you have adequate coverage if a helper or visitor should be injured during construction.

•Contractors. An uninsured contractor is a liability. Always ask for proof of insurance, and don't hire a contractor who does not have proof of coverage for workers and subcontractors.

•First-aid kit. Keep a fully stocked kit on the work site.

Here are the keys to staying within your budget: Figure an accurate estimate of the lumber and other materials you'll need, and buy only the best quality for your money.

Lumber

To calculate how much lumber you'll need for your deck, itemize all the pieces. This is called a takeoff list. Contact local suppliers to find out the available sizes and lengths, especially for any unusual pieces, such as a 3-by ledger, or lumber longer than 20 feet (most lumber is sold in 2-foot increments, from 6 to 20 feet long). Find out if certain items have special restrictions—for instance, decking lumber sold only in random lengths unless you buy a certain quantity—and find out the quantities necessary for any price breaks. You will also need to visit the supplier to personally inspect the quality of the wood.

Most construction lumber is categorized by nominal size (see page 16). Since it is the most common label, figure your estimates using nominal. A common exception is ¼-inch decking lumber, which is exactly 1¼ inches thick. But to avoid confusion and purchasing errors, be sure to verify that your supplier is working in nominal, too.

Lumber is sold by either the *lineal* or the *board* foot. Generally, construction grade lumber is sold in lineal feet. For example, a quantity of forty 2 by 8s, each 12 feet long, is referred to as 480 lineal feet (40 boards times 12 feet) of 2 by 8.

Figuring the lumber in board feet is a little more

complicated. One board foot is equal to a piece of lumber that is 12 inches wide by 12 inches long by 1 inch thick. Figuring out the board feet of a 10-foot-long 2 by 8 goes as follows: $2 \times 8 \times 120$ (length of each dimension, in inches) = 1,920 inches. Divide this total by 144 to convert it into board feet: $1,920 \div 144 = 13\frac{1}{3}$ board feet. Note that nominal dimensions are used for the thickness and width of the board.

With most suppliers, you will need to provide only the lineal dimensions of your lumber; if necessary, they will convert them into board feet for you. Always provide a complete list of the quantity and length of each dimension of lumber you need.

Choosing the species of wood that is right for your deck has a lot to do with where you live. It is a good idea to choose woods that are native to your region, or that grow fairly nearby, because you will find them readily available, reasonably priced, and best suited for your area's weather conditions. Other factors to consider are the wood's strength, workability, and durability.

Wood Grain and Defects

Grain direction is determined when raw timbers are processed at the mill. Vertical grain lines are parallel and run

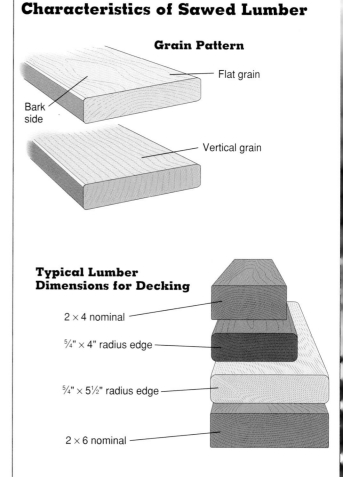

Characteristics of Sawed Lumber

Grain Pattern

Flat grain

Bark side

Vertical grain

Typical Lumber Dimensions for Decking

2 × 4 nominal

⅝" × 4" radius edge

⅝" × 5½" radius edge

2 × 6 nominal

lengthwise. A flat-grain pattern has wavy grain lines, giving it a marbled look. For decking, look for a vertical grain pattern because it is stronger and more attractive, although it is more expensive. For joists and beams, flat-grain lumber is strongest.

Lumber grades and prices are influenced by the overall condition of the wood. Natural defects and those that occur during the processing, such as splits and gouges, affect the wood's strength and workability. A better grade is more costly but generates little waste, whereas a less expensive grade requires more work

and generally produces more waste: Loose knots must be cut around, warped or twisted boards must be straightened, and pitch pockets and bark wane along the edge disfigure the wood's natural beauty.

Redwood

Although redwood is one of the more expensive woods for building decks, it is worth the price. Its straight, fine grain and texture will add a natural beauty to the finished deck, and finishes endure longer on redwood than on any other species. For its light weight, redwood is strong and durable and resists warping, yet it is

Defects to Avoid

No matter what species of wood you buy, or its grade, take the time to visually inspect each board yourself, and avoid the following defects.

•Knots. These are created where branches were originally located on the tree. Knots are weak spots and undermine a board's inherent strength.

•Checks, splits, and shakes. These are lengthwise separations along the board. Splits go all the way through the board. Checks are openings that go partially through the board, across the growth rings. Shakes are separations between growth rings that do not go completely through the board. These defects may be acceptable if they are on the board's very edge. Otherwise, there's a high risk that they will run the complete length of the board once you drill a screw or hammer a nail through it.

•Pitch pocket. An area containing pitch, it undermines the board's strength.

•Wane. A beveled edge still containing bark, it can detract from the appearance of your deck.

•Sapwood. Detected by its light color, sapwood is particularly young, or "green," and does not have the strength of mature heartwood.

•Decay. Bacteria or other live organisms slowly decompose the wood's fibers.

•Torn grain. Caused by a milling machine used to strip away the bark, it will detract from the appearance of your deck and cause splinters.

•Warp. There are three ways a board can warp: crook, a bend from end to end along its edge; bow, a bend from end to end along the face or underside; and cup, a bend from side to side across the width.

easy to saw and nail. But because it is a particularly soft wood, take care not to dent it when nailing or securing it.

You will find redwood available in several grades and lengths. Choose the lower grades, called merchantable, which have some loose knots but make excellent deck wood. For highly visible deck components and those that contact the ground, choose grades with all heartwood, which has a particularly attractive grain as well as decay resistance. If you like the look of the rose-colored heartwood, but find

the price prohibitive, consider combining it with other woods. Use the redwood for visible components, such as railings, decking, and benches, and a less expensive species or pressure-treated lumber for the structural components.

Cedar and Cypress

For homeowners who want a rustic and aged look for their deck, cedar and cypress are the popular choices. They are denser and stronger than redwood, and their burnt orange hues weather to an attractive gray.

Some woods can be left to weather naturally. Redwood (top) will eventually turn dark gray, and cedar (bottom) a silvery light gray.

Cedar and cypress are lightweight and durable, with fine, straight grain patterns and few knots. These woods—particularly their heartwood—are resistant to decay, rot, and insect infestation, and they are easy to saw and nail. However, despite their inherent strengths, cedar and cypress are not as strong as pressure-treated wood. To add to your deck's load-bearing capacity, you may want to use pressure-treated lumber for the structural components, reserving cedar or cypress for the more visible elements.

Pressure-Treated Lumber

Also known as PT lumber, pressure-treated lumber is the most common deck material used today. Like redwood, cedar, and cypress, it resists moisture, insects, and decay, but it is more readily available than those woods in most areas, and, of course, it is less expensive.

Pressure-treated lumber is medium-grade softwood—usually pine or Douglas fir—treated with preservatives to make the wood resistant to insect infestation, moisture, and decay. The often visible marks, called incisements, provide a more uniform penetration. They are not defects, so don't worry if you come across many of them. If you want lumber without the marks, you can order it without incisements.

To control shrinkage across the grain and to provide a surface that wears better, pressure-treated lumber is often quartersawed. This gives the wood a somewhat rounded appearance and reduces slightly the size of the board. Keep this in mind when figuring quantities. Use the quartersawed lumber for decking and railings, since they are exposed to the most wear and tear, as well as sun and rain.

The quality control identification stamp on pressure-treated lumber provides the year the wood was treated, the preservation chemical used, the amount of preservation retention, and the exposure condition it can withstand, such as ground contact. Always look for kiln-dried (KD) or kiln-dried after treatment (KDAT) pressure-treated lumber to assure against shrinkage and decay.

Pressure-treated wood is more economical than redwood, cypress, or cedar, but it is more difficult to saw and nail. In fact, you may need to drill pilot holes to make the nailing easier. Use power tools for sawing and drilling; it is too difficult and tiring to penetrate the wood with only hand tools. Also, avoid rip cutting (making long cuts with the grain) pressure-treated lumber, which negates the effectiveness of its chemical treatment. Coat all cuts with a wood preservative.

Before applying a finish to the deck, wait for the wood's tint to fade. This will help the paint, stain, or wood preservative adhere to the wood's surface.

You may want to ask your supplier about a new lumber that uses EPA-registered preservatives. The lumber is protected from rot and decay without the use of arsenic or chromium, and it has a water repellent built in. As it ages, it deepens to a warm brown. But don't let safety concerns deter you from using the traditional pressure-treated lumber. It makes an ideal, long-lasting, and economical deck material. The pentavalent arsenic used to preserve it is a naturally occurring element that can be found in soil, plants, animals, and even humans. In addition, the preservatives are locked into the wood and cannot migrate or evaporate. However, as with any wood, dust is produced by sawing, sanding, or drilling; the dust from pressure-treated lumber is potentially harmful if inhaled, and deserves some safety considerations. Always follow manufacturer's instructions when working with pressure-treated lumber.

Pressure-treated lumber, although resistant to decay, still requires a finish to keep it from weathering.

Nails

•*Box nails* have medium-diameter shanks and large flat heads. Their points are dulled to prevent wood from splitting. Used for general construction, they have average holding power.

•*Common nails* have thick shanks and large flat heads. Their points are dulled to prevent wood from splitting. Used for general construction, they have average holding power. A variation of the common nail is the *joist-hanger nail*, which has the same-diameter shaft as a 12d common nail but is only 1½ inches long. It is used for nailing metal framing connectors, such as joist hangers, into single pieces of 2-by lumber.

•*Finishing nails* have very thick shanks and small heads.

With only average to below average holding power, they're used specifically for attaching nonstress components. Use a nail set to countersink the dimpled head below the wood's surface, then conceal the hole with wood dough and paint.

•*Spiral-shank nails* have twisted shanks that turn like screws when driven into the wood. They have strong holding power and are not likely to lift out over time. They're excellent for preventing squeaks in decking.

•*Ring-shank nails* have a series of rings spaced along the shank; the rings lock into the wood. The nails have superior holding power but are difficult to drive and remove.

Nail Sizes, Lengths, and Counts

| Penny | | Nails (per pound) | | |
Size	Length	Common	Box	Finishing
2d	1"	875	1,000	1,350
3d	1¼"	565	635	800
4d	1½"	315	475	585
6d	2"	180	235	310
8d	2½"	105	145	190
10d	3"	70	95	120
12d	3¼"	62	90	115
16d	3½"	50	70	90
20d	4"	30	51	63
30d	4½"	23	45	—
40d	5"	17	35	—
60d	6"	11	—	—

deck builders, you will use a combination of nails, screws, bolts, and metal fasteners.

Nails

Five basic types of nails are recommended for deck construction—box, common, finishing, spiral shank, and ring shank—all available in various metals and sizes (see above). Spiral-shank or ring-shank nails have the greatest holding power.

The most popular, economical material for nails is galvanized steel, and in particular hot dipped. These corrosion-resistant nails are coated with rust-resistant zinc and are best used for structures that will be directly exposed to the elements. The nails are easily recognized by their rough gray coating. A common problem with galvanized nails is that the coating on the heads may break up when hammered. Some manufacturers double-dip the heads for added protection. Avoid nails galvanized by electrolysis rather than hot dipping. They are labeled as EG (electrogalvanized) and have

a very thin zinc coating that wears off easily.

Superior yet costly options to galvanized nails are stainless steel and solid aluminum nails. Most homeowners are not attracted to these options because the cost of stainless nails is prohibitive, and aluminum nails have less holding power and bend easily under the force of a hammer.

Nails are sized by the unlikely term of *penny*, abbreviated with a single *d* (from the ancient Roman coin the *denarius*, which was the equivalent of a penny).

If this is your first building project, the number of nails you'll need will surprise you. Be prepared to buy nails in bulk, by the pound. To determine how many pounds of nails you'll need, consult the chart above, which shows how many of each size nail are in a pound. Nails are inexpensive, so don't be afraid to overbuy. Nothing disrupts a project faster than running out of nails, and you'll always find uses for any leftovers.

Other Woods

Fir, hemlock, spruce, and pine are inexpensive and will save you money up front, but they are not necessarily the best values. They require the additional expense and work of applying finishes and preservatives, and they require extra maintenance. They also lack a natural defense against decay, and their life span is shorter.

Or you may want to include in your design such elegant woods as teak, white oak, yellow cedar, Pacific yew, and sassafras.

Finally, don't overlook "lumber" made from plastics and other synthetic products. It is durable and dimensionally stable, although more expensive than many natural woods.

It is particularly suitable for docks and waterside decks.

Hardware and Fasteners

You have a choice of a few methods of securing and connecting the deck's various components, from installing the posts to assembling the railings. Each method described here has its own merits in appearance, strength, and assembly. Some hardware and fasteners, for instance, hold tighter and longer than others, yet they take more time and effort to install. Choose the method you feel comfortable working with. In all cases, choose corrosion-resistant hardware. If you're like most

Screws

For superior holding power, screws are better than any type of nails. In addition, they allow you to easily disassemble deck components for repair or replacement. Keep in mind that driving screws takes more time and energy than driving nails, so you may want to reserve them for only the components you may need to remove in the future. Use a power driver with a bit suitable for the type of screw head to speed up the process. As with nails and other fasteners, be sure the screws are galvanized.

Other Fasteners

There are several alternatives to fastening decking boards with nails or screws, including decking clips, metal nailing

Screws and Bolts

• *Deck screws*, also known as bugle-head or multipurpose screws, have a coarsely threaded shank for excellent gripping power. The heads have flat, Phillips, square-drive (Robertson), or hexagonal configurations for driving. They do not require predrilling for countersinking; the bugle-shaped head enables them to be driven below the surface of the wood. Use a power drill with the correct style of bit. The finished look is appealing, and the holding power is superior. Use deck screws to attach decking and assemble railings and steps.

• *Lag screws* have a thicker shank than deck screws, and they have coarse threads for gripping power. One lag screw is comparable in strength to four deck screws. Lag screw heads are hexagonal shaped, and they are fastened tightly with an open-end, adjustable, or socket wrench. Holes must be predrilled. Lag screws are used to connect major structural components, such as joists and ledger boards.

• *Machine bolts* have threaded shanks and hexagonal heads, and they are used with nuts. Like lag screws, they are used for fastening major structural components, and their holes must be predrilled. They are easy to disassemble for replacement or repair.

• *Carriage bolts* are a type of machine bolt. They have rounded, nonslotted heads with square shanks just underneath, and they are secured with nuts. To insert a carriage bolt, predrill the hole so the bolt can be turned in until the square part of its shank reaches the wood. Then hammer the bolt into the wood the rest of the way. Use carriage bolts to assemble railings and posts, but be sure to keep the nuts accessible. This allows you to tighten or loosen the connection in the future.

• *Masonry bolts*, also known as expansion bolts, are used to attach the ledger board to a masonry wall. The bolt includes a sleeve you are to insert into a predrilled hole in the masonry wall. The sleeve then expands as the bolt turns, for a secure fit. Masonry bolts come with either a head or a threaded end for use with a nut.

• *Malleable washers* are thick, heavy washers used with lag screws, machine bolts, and carriage bolts in holding wood structures together. They have two finishes: black iron, which will rust, and galvanized iron, which is rust resistant.

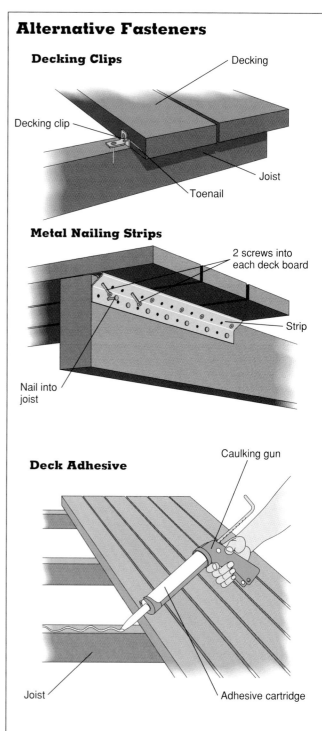

Alternative Fasteners

Decking Clips

Decking

Decking clip

Joist

Toenail

Metal Nailing Strips

2 screws into each deck board

Strip

Nail into joist

Deck Adhesive

Caulking gun

Joist

Adhesive cartridge

strips, and deck adhesive (a type of outdoor construction adhesive). All three systems are intended to fasten the boards with no nail heads or screw heads on the surface, avoiding a pathway for water and eventual rot. (Also see page 66.)

Decking clips, which are nailed along one edge of a board before it is set in place, secure that edge with small flanges that slip under the previously installed board; the free edge of the board is held in place with traditional toe-nailing through the side. The clips create uniform spacing between the boards. Some models have teeth or claws to grip the decking.

Metal fastening strips, which are laid on top of joists, are secured with nails into the sides of the joists; screws are then driven up through predrilled holes in the strip into the bottoms of the decking boards.

Deck adhesive, applied with a caulking gun, is an invisible method of fastening the decking boards to the joists. Although it makes the decking smooth and attractive, there is one important drawback you should consider. Once the adhesive sets up, it's almost impossible to remove the decking boards without damaging them and the joists to which they are fastened. It is also difficult to use adhesive to install bowed boards.

Metal Framing Connectors

Framing connectors simplify the assembly of components, and they strengthen connections. Building codes may

Connectors Used for Deck Framing

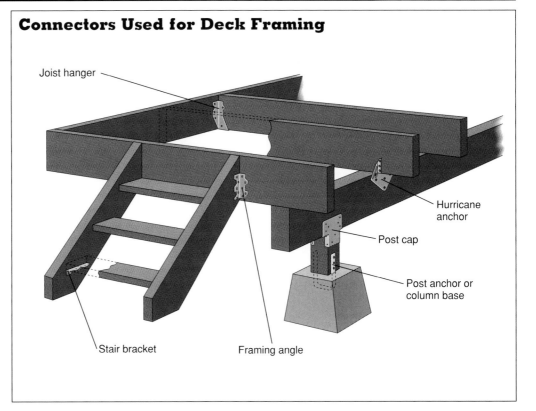

Joist hanger
Hurricane anchor
Post cap
Post anchor or column base
Stair bracket
Framing angle

Metal Framing Connectors

A full catalog of framing connectors contains dozens of sizes, shapes, and configurations, for almost any framing connection imaginable. Here are the types most appropriate for deck construction.

•*Framing angles*, or reinforcing angles, create a solid and strong joint between two framing members, such as an end joist and a joist header.

•*Straps* are general-purpose metal fasteners used to strengthen joints. They can be straight, T shaped, or L shaped, to fit various joints.

•*Stair angles* are metal brackets, in an angle shape, used to attach treads to straight, or solid, stringers. They are easy to install, very

strong, and available in a variety of lengths.

•*Joist hangers* connect the joists to the header, beam, or ledger board, and provide support. They are superior in strength to other methods of attachment. Because the side flanges are nailed into 2-by lumber with no other lumber behind it, they require short, thick nails, referred to as joist-hanger nails.

•*Post caps,* which connect posts and beams, are available in one- or two-piece styles. Use them to secure cross beams on top of posts. The two-piece style is used after the beam is already positioned; once the post cap is installed, it is not possible to disassemble the cross beams.

•*Post anchors* and *column bases* are used to attach or anchor the posts to concrete piers. They are placed in the concrete just after pouring. Elevated models are designed to raise the posts above the pier and protect them from standing water. Anchors prevent the post from splitting, and they replace toenailing. They are also available in height-adjustable models.

•*Hurricane anchors*, also called seismic anchors, are strong metal connectors that can hold joists to beams, trusses to rafters, or any two intersecting structural components. For deck construction, they are useful for attaching joists to beams.

specify that connectors be used to reinforce certain joints, such as the connection between a post and a beam, or between a joist and a ledger board. Framing connectors also help prevent wood from splitting when nailed, and reduce dents or dimples by acting as a barrier between the wood and hammer head. The connectors are sized to accommodate standard-dimension wood; some connectors have optional sizes for full-cut (rough) lumber and for built-up members (two 2 by 4s nailed together, for instance). Be sure that the fasteners are galvanized to prevent rust. Follow the manufacturer's recommendations for nailing and bolting; some connections require that full-sized nails, rather than the shorter joist-hanger nails, be used, or that all holes have nails.

Concrete

In deck projects, concrete serves two purposes. Concrete footings and piers provide a durable foundation for the deck, and concrete slabs create adjoining stair landings, walkways, and patios.

The amount of concrete you'll need depends on the number and depth of the footings you plan to pour. This in turn depends on the local building codes and the size of your deck. When you order concrete, include any you'll need for a walkway or patio.

You can order ready-to-pour concrete from a supplier, but for a small job such as pouring a few footings, it's more economical to mix your own. You'll need cement, sand, and gravel. You might

Concrete for Footings

The basic units for measuring concrete are the cubic foot and cubic yard (27 cubic feet). To calculate the amount of concrete you need for footings, first figure out the volume of each hole. If the hole is round, the formula for the volume of a circle (πr^2) can be used with a simple modification: Volume = $\pi r^2 \times$ depth of hole. $\pi = 3.1416$ and r = radius of the hole at its widest point. If you take all measurements in inches, divide the total by 1,728, the number of cubic inches in a cubic foot. Otherwise, take all measurements in fractions of a foot (for example, 18 inches is 1½ feet).

To illustrate, consider 24 footing holes that are 10 inches wide and 24 inches deep. The radius is one half the distance across, or 5 inches. Multiply 3.1416 times 5^2 times 24, or 3.1416 times 25 times 24, to get 1,884.96 cubic inches. Divide this by 1,728 to get 1.09 cubic feet per footing hole. Multiply by 24 footing holes to get 26.16 total cubic feet of concrete, which is very close to a yard (27 cubic feet). Be sure to add an allowance for widened footings.

The label on each bag of concrete or mix states how much concrete it will make. Divide that amount into your

total requirements to get the total number of bags you will need for the footing holes.

To figure how much concrete you'll need for a walkway, find the volume by multiplying the length of the walkway by the width by the depth, all measured in inches. To find the amount of concrete you'll need in cubic feet, divide the volume by 1,728 (cubic inches in a cubic foot).

To convert cubic feet into cubic yards for large jobs, figure the total volume of concrete in cubic feet, then divide by 27 (cubic feet in a cubic yard). For example, 135 cubic feet ÷ 27 = 5 cubic yards.

Calculating Volume of Footing and Pier

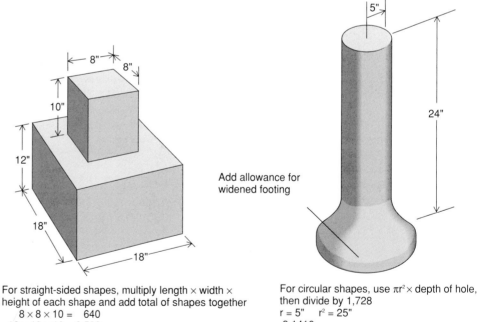

For straight-sided shapes, multiply length × width × height of each shape and add total of shapes together

$$8 \times 8 \times 10 = 640$$
$$+12 \times 18 \times 18 = \underline{2,592}$$
$$3,232$$

Then divide by 1,728 to get cubic feet = 1.87

Add allowance for widened footing

For circular shapes, use $\pi r^2 \times$ depth of hole, then divide by 1,728

r = 5" r^2 = 25"

$$3.1416$$
$$\times 25$$
$$\overline{78.5}$$
$$\times 24$$
$$\overline{1,885} \div 1,728 = 1.09 + 0.1 \text{ for footing} =$$
1.19 cubic feet

also consider renting a portable mixer instead of mixing individual batches in a wheelbarrow, trough, or tub (see page 54).

If you don't want to mix your own, look for ready-to-use concrete mix at your local home-improvement store. It is a little more expensive than mixing your own, but it eliminates figuring and buying the individual ingredients. All the dry ingredients come pre-mixed in one bag; just add water and combine.

In order to buy the proper amount of ingredients or cement mix, you must know how to convert cubic inches into cubic feet and cubic yards. Whether you are buying ready-mix cement or the ingredients to mix your own, read the manufacturer's label carefully to figure the exact number of bags you'll need.

Other Supplies

Lumber, concrete, and fasteners are not all you'll need to build your deck. To install the ledger board, you will need flashing or spacer blocks, and silicone caulk. Depending on your deck's site, you might also need perforated drainpipe or flexible tubing, drain rock, and landscaping felt for proper drainage, and weed-control fabric to inhibit weed growth. You may need reinforcing steel and fiber forming tubes for the footings.

If you plan to add accessories such as special lighting, electrical outlets, and plumbing connections for a sink, spa, or plant watering system, buy the supplies you'll need for roughing in the electrical, plumbing,

and lighting installations, even if you will not complete these additions until later.

You may want to buy precast concrete piers rather than form and pour your own concrete piers (you will still need to pour concrete footings for the precast piers). Some piers come with brackets, which are superior to the type with wood blocks on top. Another type of pier has preformed grooves on the top, into which posts or joists are slipped.

Tips for Buying, Ordering, and Storing Materials

Now that you've figured your materials, do you buy them as needed or all at once? If you buy as needed, you'll spend a lot of time making trips to suppliers, but you won't have to store large quantities of materials or invest a large amount of money up front. If you've carefully broken down the large tasks into small ones while you were setting up your budget, you already know exactly what you need and when you'll need it.

However, buying all the materials at once has advantages. You'll save time on the shopping, and you can save money, too. Some suppliers offer volume discounts and free delivery for large orders.

Before you leave the store, inspect the materials closely for damage. When buying lumber, always choose and inspect each piece yourself. Expect slight variations in quality within a shipment, but be sure the lot is what you

Other Supplies
- Forming tube
- Precast pier with post anchor
- Pier with slots
- Weed-control fabric
- Perforated drainpipe
- Caulk
- Caulking gun
- Drain rock
- 6" metal flashing
- Spacer blocks
- Electrical supplies

want. Most lumber today is second-growth and fast-growth wood, which is often not as dense and durable as first-growth, or virgin, lumber.

Pay attention to the manufacturer's labels on the materials. They provide valuable information about the product's uses, coverages, and shelf life. Safety information on the label protects you. Follow it. Read the cautions regarding handling, storage, and proper disposal of leftovers.

Avoid special-order items, especially if you're new to construction. Generally, these items are more expensive, so it's best to design your deck using standard, readily available materials. If you do plan to use special-order items, however, plan ahead. Obtain cost estimates and the lead time for ordering. Once you

place your order, check regularly on its status. Have a contingency plan in case the item is delayed or not available.

Transporting large, heavy lumber and materials is a major concern. It's dangerous to load up your car with long and large materials. Unless you have access to a truck with a sturdy lumber rack, make arrangements for the supplier to deliver the items. Some suppliers charge a nominal fee for deliveries or offer free delivery with large orders. When loading and unloading heavy or bulky items, don't attempt to do it by yourself. Get a helper.

Prior to delivery, choose and plan the storage area. Select a secure site that is close to the work site and easily accessible. As the materials are unloaded, organize and stack them carefully.

BUILDING YOUR DECK

Now that you have a set of plans and have completed the critical preparation tasks, you are ready to start construction. If you planned carefully, building your deck will be an enjoyable and rewarding experience; you're not likely to make any serious mistakes—although you should expect a few small ones—and construction should move along smoothly.

This chapter presents step-by-step instructions for building a basic deck. Some of the steps include variations of certain tasks. Depending on your deck design, site requirements, local codes, and personal experience, you may prefer an alternative method, or even choose to alter the order of the steps. If so, jot down notes or mark passages as you read through the chapter, for easier reference during construction.

If you plan to hire a contractor to do all or part of the work, this chapter will give you an understanding of the construction process, so you will be able to communicate clearly your needs and concerns.

A deck may take from one weekend to several weeks to build. If your building site is steep, figure that it will take twice the effort that a flat site would.

SITE PREPARATION AND LAYOUT

Preparing the site is the first step in the construction process. The amount of work involved depends on the extent of the alterations you must make to your house, as well as the condition of the site itself. Once the site is cleared, graded, and ready, you can install the ledger and lay out string lines for the post locations.

Step 1: Prepare the Site

Begin preparing the site by measuring and marking off the overall deck area and the approximate location of the posts, using stakes and string. At this stage you can use rough estimates, unless there are specific obstacles or underground conditions that you are concerned about. If so, see Step 3 on page 47 for techniques for laying out an accurate string outline, which will aid you in pinpointing critical locations on the site. If you aren't certain about property line locations, easements, setbacks, or other site legalities, hire a surveyor to verify them.

Elements of a Deck

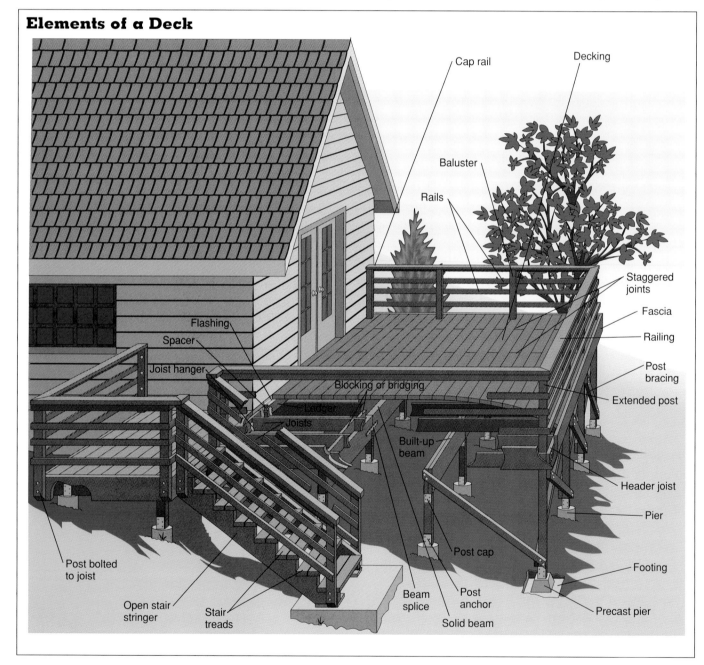

- Cap rail
- Decking
- Baluster
- Rails
- Staggered joints
- Fascia
- Railing
- Flashing
- Spacer
- Joist hanger
- Blocking or bridging
- Ledger
- Joists
- Post bracing
- Extended post
- Built-up beam
- Header joist
- Pier
- Post cap
- Post bolted to joist
- Beam splice
- Post anchor
- Footing
- Open stair stringer
- Stair treads
- Solid beam
- Precast pier

Now is the time to buy that "ounce of prevention."

Part of site preparation is making any necessary repairs or alterations to the house. These include painting siding or trim that the deck will cover; adjusting gutters and relocating downspouts to rechannel water away from the ground below the deck and to get downspouts out of the way of the ledger board; removing any attached structures, such as a porch or stairs, that are in the way of the deck; and removing, relocating, or installing doors and windows as necessary. Complete as much of this work as possible before deck construction begins; however, if your plan includes a new door, wait to install it until after the deck is built.

If the deck site is covered by an existing patio, as long as it slopes away from the house, you can simply build over it. You will have to break holes through the patio to excavate for the deck footings, but leaving the rest of it in place makes it easier to control weeds, clutter, dust, and moisture. If the patio slopes toward the house or interferes with the deck's design and structure, break it up and remove the pieces. You may find uses for the broken concrete in your garden, or someone else may be able to use it, in which case they should haul it away for free.

Grading

Take a careful look at the ground of the deck site. Does it slope away from the house? Are there minor rises, dips, and other irregularities? It

may be necessary for you to smooth and slope, or grade, the site in order to improve surface drainage. This may simply be a matter of moving soil from one area to another, or it may require bringing in or removing extra soil. You may be able to do this by hand, but if the site requires extensive excavation, you should consider hiring an excavation contractor who can

complete the work quickly and neatly, or you may want to rent a minitractor with a front loader. If it's a major job, both are well worth the price. If you tackle the job yourself, try to avoid the areas where the footings or posts will be located. Disturbed soil is less stable and may allow the posts or concrete to shift. If you have to add fill to those areas, plan to excavate the footing

holes proportionately deeper. Likewise, if you are building the deck on a filled site, consult with a soils engineer or deck contractor.

Providing Drainage

You will also need to evaluate the site for adequate drainage. Poor drainage causes standing water, which accelerates wood

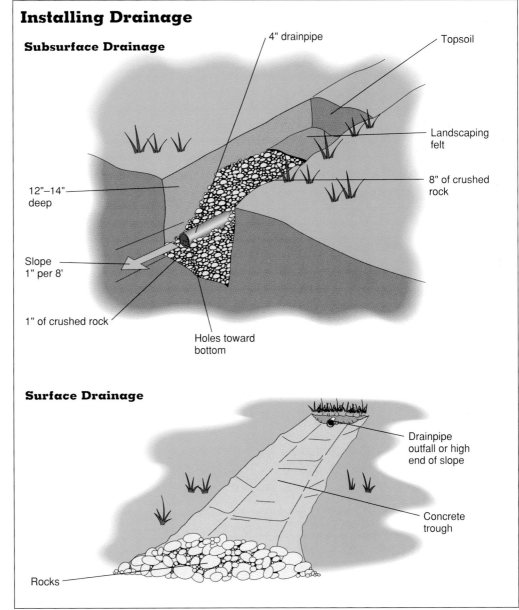

Installing Drainage

Subsurface Drainage

4" drainpipe

Topsoil

Landscaping felt

8" of crushed rock

12"–14" deep

Slope 1" per 8'

1" of crushed rock

Holes toward bottom

Surface Drainage

Drainpipe outfall or high end of slope

Concrete trough

Rocks

decay and tends to become a breeding ground for mosquitoes and other insects. Proper drainage helps stabilize the soil and prevents erosion, which can cause the deck to shift.

To control water runoff, you can provide surface drainage to divert water around the deck area. To control standing water, you will need to build a subsurface drainage system that will channel the water away from the deck and disperse it properly, away from any other structures.

For subsurface drainage, start by determining the direction in which you want the water runoff to go, then locate the nearest low point on your property where water can be dispersed. Keep in mind that you cannot drain water onto your neighbor's property. If you have no appropriate spot, you may need to divert the water into a drywell—a hole 4 feet in diameter and 4 to 6 feet deep, filled with rocks and gravel.

If you do have a suitable low point, create a drainage ditch by digging a 12- to 14-inch-deep trench that runs from the deck site to the low point. The ditch should slope ⅛ inch per foot, or 1 inch every 8 feet. Spread a 1-inch bed of gravel or crushed stone in the trench. Cut or piece together, as necessary, 4-inch-diameter drainpipe—either rigid polyvinyl chloride (PVC) or acrylonitrile-butadiene-styrene (ABS) pipe, or flexible polyethylene tubing—with one or two rows of holes along one side. Place the pipe in the trench, on the gravel, with the perforations close to but

not on the bottom (skewed approximately 30 degrees). Cover the pipe with an additional 8 inches of gravel. To prevent dirt from clogging the gravel and pipe, cover the gravel with a layer of landscaping felt. This water-permeable barrier holds the soil in place yet allows water to filter through. Finish by filling the trench with soil to match the existing grade.

If you anticipate a large amount of runoff, form a gravel or concrete trough at the exit point of the drainage pipe to further disperse the water, sloping it 1 inch for every 8 feet.

Controlling Weeds and Grass

To prevent weeds, grass, and other vegetation from growing under the deck, clear the area and then cover it with a weed-control fabric, which blocks sunlight and, unlike polyethylene sheeting, allows moisture to pass through it into the ground rather than allowing it to accumulate in puddles. Use as large a piece as possible to minimize seams, which will eventually stretch out of place.

Cover the fabric with about an inch of sand or small gravel. Use heavy rocks to hold the fabric in place while you do this. When you must walk over the covered area, do so carefully, to prevent tears and rips. If the area under the deck will be visible, you may want to spread a layer of mulch over the sand or gravel to give it a more finished look.

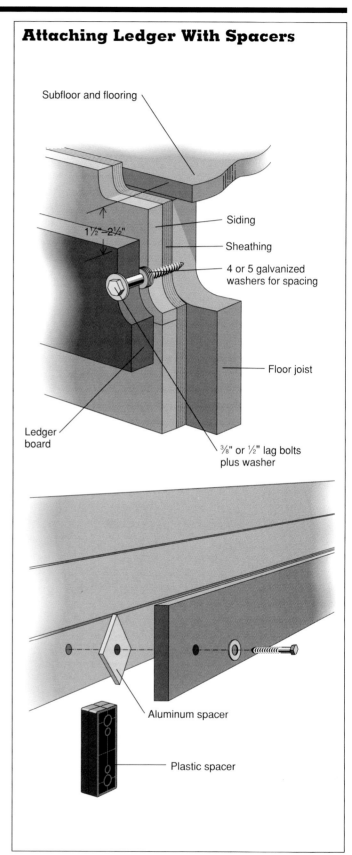

Attaching Ledger With Spacers

Subfloor and flooring

1½"–2½"

Siding

Sheathing

4 or 5 galvanized washers for spacing

Floor joist

Ledger board

⅜" or ½" lag bolts plus washer

Aluminum spacer

Plastic spacer

Attaching Ledger With Flashing

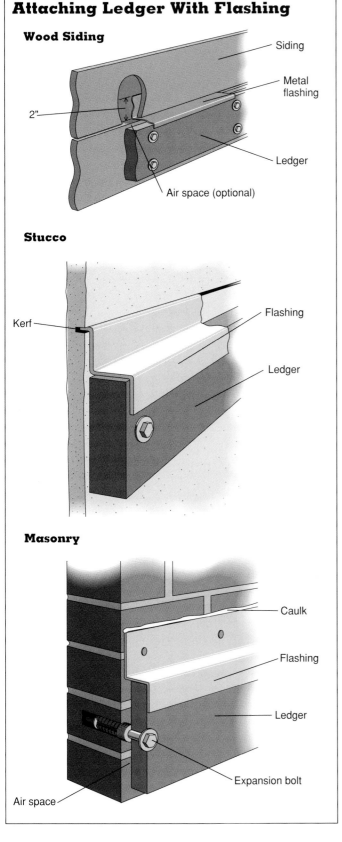

Wood Siding

Siding

Metal flashing

2"

Ledger

Air space (optional)

Stucco

Kerf

Flashing

Ledger

Masonry

Caulk

Flashing

Ledger

Expansion bolt

Air space

Step 2: Install the Ledger Board

The ledger is the major structural component that connects the deck to the house. It supports up to half of the deck load, so selecting the board, providing moisture protection, and attaching the ledger securely to the house are all critical tasks. Although you can install the ledger board after the footings are in, installing it before layout makes layout easier and more accurate. Note: This step applies only if your deck is attached to the house. If you are building a stand-alone deck, proceed to Step 3.

Selecting and Measuring the Ledger Board

When buying lumber for the deck, hand-select one piece specifically for the ledger board. It must be straight, and its top edge should be free of knots. Select the piece from pressure-treated lumber or all-heart construction grade lumber of a durable species. Most ledgers are one size wider than the joists (a 2 by 8 ledger for 2 by 6 joists, for instance) or slightly thicker than the joists (unsurfaced lumber for the ledger, surfaced for the joists). Check your local building code for precise requirements.

The length of the ledger board depends on how the end joists are attached. If you use joist hangers, make the board at least 3 inches longer than the outside-of-joist-to-

outside-of-joist framing dimension. If you bolt the two outside joists against the ends of the ledger, shorten the board by the width of the joists. After cutting the ledger board to length, apply preservative to the cut end.

Preventing Trapped Moisture

The back of the ledger board must be protected from moisture and rot. For most areas, and for most types of siding, the easiest and most reliable way to prevent moisture from being trapped is to provide a ½-inch air space between the ledger board and the house, using galvanized washers, aluminum or plastic spacer blocks, or other rust-resistant spacers; do not use wood for spacers.

If the deck will be subjected to constant moisture (on the shady side of a house in a humid climate, for instance), or if the siding is a material that retains moisture (such as brick), the ledger should be protected by metal flashing. Cut the flashing to the length of the ledger board and secure it to the house wall. For horizontal board siding, loosen the board above the ledger, tuck the flashing at least 2 inches under the siding, and bend the flashing down over the ledger. For a masonry wall, secure the flashing with masonry nails. First, run a bead of silicone caulk behind the flashing. Then bend the flashing over the ledger, run another bead of caulk along the top edge of the flashing, and caulk the nail heads. For stucco, cut a groove, or kerf, in the wall, using a circular saw with a masonry blade. Then run a bead of caulk into the groove, tuck the top edge of the flashing into it, and bend the flashing down on top of the ledger board. In this case, do not nail or screw the flashing; it will be held in place by the first decking board.

Positioning and Attaching the Ledger

Mark a level line on the house wall for the top of the ledger board. This line should be 1½ to 2½ inches below the house floor level, to make the deck surface even with the interior floor—allowing for the thickness of the deck boards—and to keep rainwater and melted snow from seeping under doors.

There are three ways to make the ledger board level: Use a long level to scribe a series of straight, level lines linked to each other; hold (with a helper) a long straightedge in place, with a level on top, and scribe along it; or use a hydro level or builder's level to establish two level end points for the line and snap a chalk line between them.

The method of fastening the ledger board to the house depends on the house structure, the type of siding material, and the method you will use to prevent moisture from getting trapped behind the ledger.

Wood-Frame Wall

Attach the ledger with carriage bolts or lag screws, and malleable washers (heavy washers that distribute pressure better than ordinary cut washers). The bolts or lag

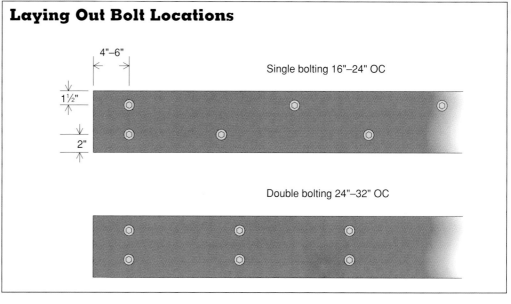

Laying Out Bolt Locations

4"–6"

Single bolting 16"–24" OC

1½"

2"

Double bolting 24"–32" OC

screws must be at least ⅜ inch in diameter and must connect to the framing behind the siding. Lag screws should penetrate the framing according to local code requirements (typically, 3 inches). If you have access beneath the house, use carriage bolts or machine bolts, and nuts.

First, using a tape measure and square, lay out the bolt hole locations on the ledger board. Locate two bolts one above the other, 4 to 6 inches from each end of the board; then place single bolts every 16 to 24 inches, staggered top and bottom, or double bolts every 24 to 32 inches. (If the deck is at a height other than floor level, mark the hole locations where they will align with the wall studs.) The bolts should be at least 2 inches from the bottom edge of the ledger and 1½ inches from its top edge. Drill the holes with a bit ⅛ inch larger than the diameter of the bolts you will use.

To drill holes into the house wall, position the ledger temporarily with bracing or with 16d duplex nails. Using the holes in the ledger as guides, drill pilot holes for lag screws through the siding and into the framing. Drill through the siding and sheathing with the same bit you used for the ledger holes; then drill into the framing, just far enough for the lag screw tip to reach, with a smaller-sized bit (¼-inch bit for ⅜-inch lag screws, ⁵⁄₁₆-inch bit for ½-inch screws). If you are using carriage bolts, drill the bolt holes all the way through the floor joist or the blocking, using the same diameter bit as for the ledger.

To secure the ledger, first pull it from the wall and dab silicone caulk into each pilot hole in the wall. With the ledger board standing on edge, slide the bolts or lag screws, with washers, through the ledger holes; then slip on the spacers, position the board, and tighten the bolts.

To drill holes into a stucco wall, transfer the hole locations from the ledger board onto the wall with a pencil. Remove the ledger board. Using a masonry bit, drill only through the stucco. Then change to wood bits to drill shank holes through the sheathing and narrower pilot holes into the framing. Dab silicone caulk into the holes. Slip the lag screws, washers, and spacers onto the ledger board, position the board, and tighten the screws. If flashing is required, saw the kerf into the stucco before bolting the ledger in place.

For vinyl or aluminum siding, or for board siding where you want to install metal flashing, you'll need to remove some of the siding before installing the ledger board. First, mark cutting lines on the wall where the ledger will go. (Add space at both ends for end joists that go outside the ledger board.) Use snips to cut aluminum or vinyl siding, taking small "bites" to keep the cut straight

Bolting Ledger to Wall

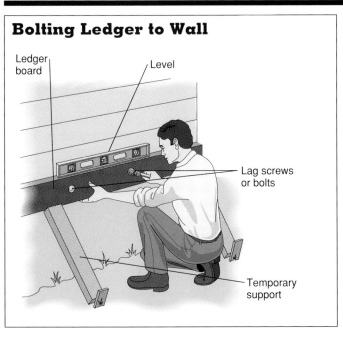

Ledger board
Level
Lag screws or bolts
Temporary support

Removing Vinyl or Aluminum Siding

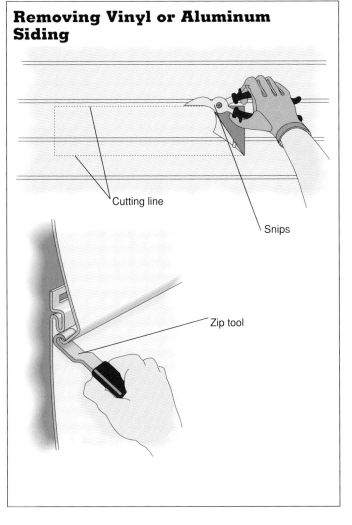

Cutting line
Snips
Zip tool

and even. You can also cut vinyl with several passes of a utility knife against a straight-edge, and unlock panels at a joint with a special "zip tool." To cut away wood siding, use a circular saw with the blade depth set at only the thickness of the siding; then use a compass saw or chisel to finish the cutout. Cut a piece of 5- or 6-inch-wide aluminum flashing to the length of the cutout, slide the flashing under the siding to a snug fit, and bend the flashing up to make room for the ledger. Install the ledger. Then, using a scrap of wood and a hammer, bend the flashing down over the front edge of the ledger.

Masonry, Brick, or Concrete Wall

To attach the ledger board to brick, masonry, or concrete, use masonry expansion bolts or lead shields with lag screws. For these materials, the holes in the wall are drilled first, then the holes in the ledger board are drilled. To begin, using the level lay-out line for reference, measure and mark the positions of the anchors on the wall: two holes every 24 inches. Using a rotary hammer and masonry bit, drill these holes. To clear the dust out of each hole, insert plastic tubing into the hole and blow through it (protect your eyes). Drive the lead shields or anchors into the holes.

To mark the hole locations on the ledger board, brace the board in position on the wall and hammer the face of the board so that the anchors protruding from the wall make indentations on the back. Take down the ledger board and

drill the holes at these marks. Insert the lag screws through the holes (with malleable washers), slide the spacers onto them, and screw them into the anchors.

Step 3: Lay Out Post Locations

There are two reasons for an accurate deck layout. First, it ensures that the four corners of a basic rectangular deck will each be exactly 90°. It also ensures that the posts are placed accurately, so the footings, beams, joists, and decking will be in proper position. The best way to square the deck and align the posts is to lay out temporary string lines that delineate the post locations. Although you could lay out the string lines to delineate the deck platform itself, and take measurements from those lines for the locations of the posts and footings, it simplifies construction to lay out lines for only the posts. Other measurements, such as footing excavations or beam lengths, can be taken from them.

The starting point for a layout is the ledger board. If the ledger board is not in place and you don't plan to install it until after pouring the concrete footings, lay out the top line of the ledger board on the house to use as a reference for laying out post locations (see pages 48 and 49). Be sure to allow for the thickness of the ledger board, as well as for the spacers you may be planning to use, when measuring and marking for the layout. Note: For a stand-alone deck, batter boards take the place of the ledger board.

Building Batter Boards

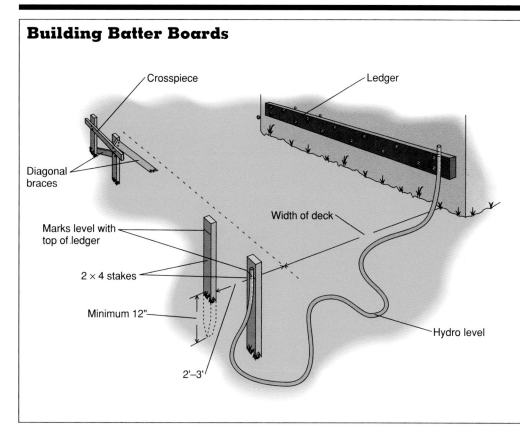

Crosspiece

Ledger

Diagonal braces

Marks level with top of ledger

2 × 4 stakes

Minimum 12"

Width of deck

Hydro level

2'–3'

Building Batter Boards

Note on your plans where the outside edges of the two outside posts are located in relation to the ledger board—that is, whether they are flush with the outside edge of the ledger board or set in a few inches. Drive a 6d nail into the top of the ledger board at each of these locations and tie the end of a string to each one. Use mason's nylon twine, not cotton string.

Measure from the ledger board, across what will be the width of the deck, to the farthest posts. With a helper, and using a framing square placed against the ledger board to keep the strings at right angles to the ledger, stretch each string 2 to 3 feet beyond that point. There you will need

to set up temporary braces to support string lines as you align and adjust them. You may be able to nail a 2 by 4 crosspiece to a nearby fence, wall, or other yard structure. If not, create batter boards: Sharpen a pair of 2 by 4 stakes for each batter board and drive them into the ground 12 inches, parallel with the ledger and 2 to 3 feet apart. They should be at least as high as the ledger.

Using a hydro level, or a long straightedge with a level, or a builder's level, or a line level, mark on each stake (or fence, shed, wall, etc.) the point that is exactly level with the top of the ledger board. With 16d duplex nails, nail a 3- to 4-foot 2 by 4 crosspiece to the stakes (or fence, etc.) so the top is even with the marks,

attaching it to the sides of the stakes facing away from the ledger board. Brace the stakes diagonally with a 1-by piece of scrap lumber. Stretch out each string line again and drive a 6d nail into the top of each crosspiece where the line crosses over it; tie the strings to the nails.

Next, build batter boards for a third string line that will cross the first two at right angles on a line marking the outside edges of the posts. This line should be level with the other two. If there are additional rows of posts parallel with this one, lay out a string line for each row.

Note: Where batter boards for a high deck are not feasible, and there are no high structures convenient enough for attaching string lines,

move the layout grid closer to the ground. Make sure that it is level and that the corners under the ledger board are aligned plumb with the ledger board marks.

Squaring the String Lines

Once the string lines are in place, you must adjust them so they are absolutely square to each other and to the ledger board, forming a perfect right angle at each intersection. There are two ways to do this. One way, for a simple rectangular deck, is to measure the diagonals (measure the distances between opposite corners). The two measurements should be equal; adjust the string lines until they are, moving the nails on the batter boards to the final positions.

Another way to establish square corners is with a 3—4—5 triangle. Multiples of 3, 4, and 5, such as 6—8—10, 9—12—15, or similar sets, can be used with measurements in feet or yards. To form the triangle with these three numbers, measure 3 feet from the corner along one line and 4 feet along the other line; then measure the distance between the two points. It should be 5 feet. If not, pivot one of the lines until the measurement is precisely 5 feet.

With the string lines level and square, transfer the post positions from your plans to the ground. Keep in mind that the string lines indicate the outside faces of posts. Using a plumb bob and tape measure, find where the center of each post will be, and drive a small stake into the ground at that point.

Layout for a Deck

Squaring String Lines

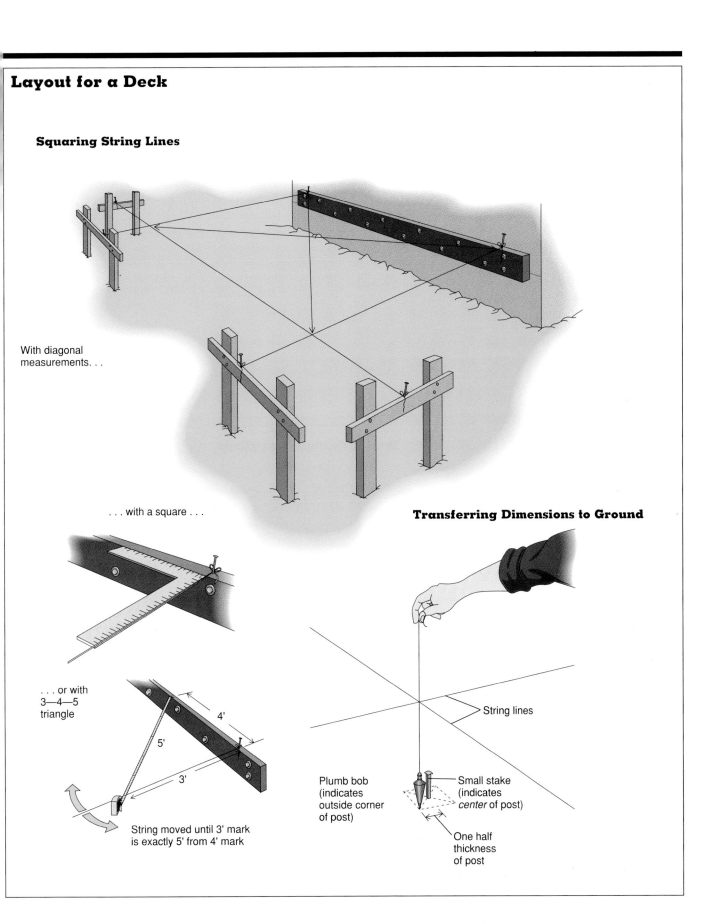

With diagonal measurements. . .

. . . with a square . . .

. . . or with 3—4—5 triangle

4'

5'

3'

String moved until 3' mark is exactly 5' from 4' mark

Transferring Dimensions to Ground

String lines

Plumb bob (indicates outside corner of post)

Small stake (indicates *center* of post)

One half thickness of post

Most foundations for deck posts consist of a buried concrete footing that supports a concrete pier, although some deck posts are buried directly in the ground. Whichever type you build, you will have to dig holes for the footings, and mix and pour some concrete.

Step 4: Dig the Holes

The depth of the footing holes depends on local soil conditions and the frost line in your area. Typically, the minimum depth in areas with mild climates is 12 inches on flat sites, 18 inches on slopes. In areas with cold climates, the holes should be deep enough so the footings sit below the frost line on a 6-inch bed of gravel. Verify the required depth and width of footings with your local building department, and consult with local utility companies about any digging restrictions they may have, especially near property lines.

For shallow footings (18 inches or less), excavate the hole to the same width as the footings, which usually vary from 12 to 18 inches square. For deeper excavations, make the width of the hole the same as the minimum diameter for the pier; then enlarge the bottom of the hole to the required footing width. If the soil is not stable enough to hold this bell-bottom shape, excavate a wider hole and build a form for the pier with a fiber forming tube (see page 52).

To begin, mark an outline on the ground for each hole, using the layout stakes as guides. A quick way to make outlines is to cut a cardboard template to the size of the footing excavations, with a small hole in the exact center. Lay the template on the ground so the hole fits over the layout stake, and sprinkle ordinary flour around the perimeter. Be sure that the stakes represent the center of each post, not an edge. If the template is a square, be sure to align its edges parallel to the layout lines. Remove the layout lines temporarily for digging.

To dig, use a posthole, or clamshell, digger. Unlike a shovel, it removes dirt without disturbing the surrounding area and leaves smoothly shaved holes with firm sides. Use a square-nosed shovel for squaring the sides and shaping the bottom of the hole, which must be level and have squared (not rounded) edges where the sides meet the bottom. For a large job, consider renting a power auger, or hire a professional. The auger resembles a huge power drill; it is gasoline powered and is best operated by two people.

In the process of digging, you'll come across rocks and roots. Have handy a pry bar and wrecking bar to break up rocks, as well as an ax or a pruning saw to cut away roots. Place all excavated dirt (it will be a sizable amount) far enough away from the holes so it won't interfere with construction. If any batter boards are disturbed, restring the layout lines immediately and check their squareness by measuring diagonals.

Digging Holes

Marking the Ground

Stake indicating center of post
Flour
Paper template

Typical Footing Dimensions

Post anchor
Pier
8"
8" min.
Footing
Square edges
12" min. (varies)
Level bottom
6"
Batter board
18" (varies)
Gravel (optional)

Excavating

Batter board
Batter board
Layout lines
Posthole digger

Options for Supporting Posts

There are several methods of supporting deck posts, depending on the deck design and local building requirements. These are the most common options.

•Post attached above grade: The post is attached to a footing, a pier, or a footing-and-pier combination 6 to 8 inches above ground level, using post anchors. This is the preferred method, because the post doesn't come in contact with the ground or standing water. The posts will last longer and will be easier to replace, if necessary, than if they were buried in the ground. Use pressure-treated or heart construction grade lumber, or a durable species. If you use precast piers, choose the type with a metal post bracket, not a wood nailing block.

•Post buried in ground: The post is attached to a concrete footing below ground level, using post anchors. The post must be pressure-treated lumber specified for burial or ground contact, to prevent moisture and insect damage. Posts attached in this manner are very rigid and eliminate the need for concrete footings. However, they are more difficult to replace, and because they are exposed to the moisture in the ground, they have a shorter life span.

•Post cast in concrete: The post is buried and concrete poured around it. No pier is used. The post must be pressure-treated lumber specified for burial or ground contact. This installation is more stable than a post buried directly in the ground, but replacing the post is extremely difficult; it also has a relatively short life span.

•Beam attached to footing: No posts or piers are required. Pressure-treated beams attach directly to metal anchors embedded in concrete footings. This is a very stable method of securing the deck: There are no posts that need bracing, and the beams do not contact the ground or standing water. This method requires accurate layout and pier construction, because the piers and anchor brackets for each beam must be perfectly level with each other.

Pier and Post Options

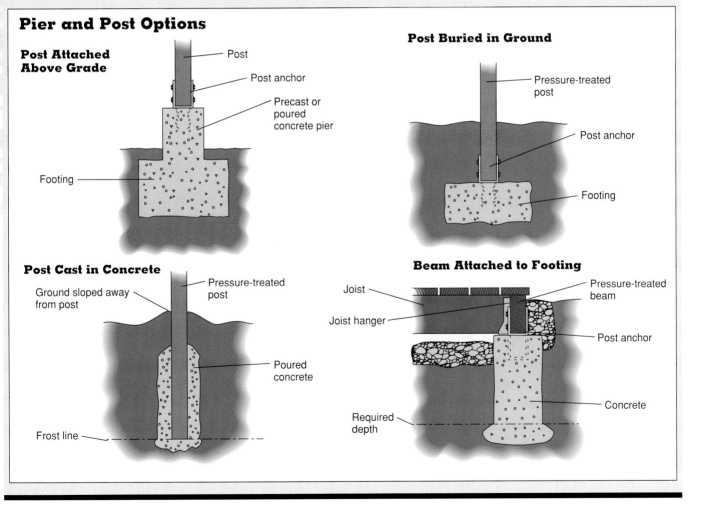

Post Attached Above Grade
- Post
- Post anchor
- Precast or poured concrete pier
- Footing

Post Buried in Ground
- Pressure-treated post
- Post anchor
- Footing

Post Cast in Concrete
- Ground sloped away from post
- Pressure-treated post
- Poured concrete
- Frost line

Beam Attached to Footing
- Joist
- Joist hanger
- Pressure-treated beam
- Post anchor
- Concrete
- Required depth

Step 5: Mix and Pour the Concrete

The simplest foundation is made by setting a precast pier in a poured concrete footing, but if footings are deeper than 12 inches, or if you want to customize the appearance of the piers, or if you want to tie the footing and pier together with rebar, you should cast the piers and footings as one unit.

Whether you use precast piers or pour your own, you'll need to mix and pour some concrete for the footings (see page 54). If you estimate that you'll need more than ½ yard (14 cubic feet, or 10 wheel-barrows) of concrete, you may want to order a delivery of ready-mixed concrete. Be sure to have the holes and any forms or reinforcing steel in-spected before you pour the concrete.

Pouring the Footings and Piers

The easiest way to form piers is with fiber forming tubes, available from most concrete suppliers and many lumber yards. (You can also nail to-gether four-sided forms made from scrap lumber; reinforce the forms for large piers by wrapping them tightly with wire.) Tubes come in various diameters; most deck piers require 8-inch tubes. Estimate the height of all the piers (see the next sentence) and buy a tube long enough for the total, plus an extra foot or two. With a handsaw or power circular saw, cut the tube for each pier to length, so the top will be 8 inches above grade and the

Mixing Concrete

Proportioning Materials

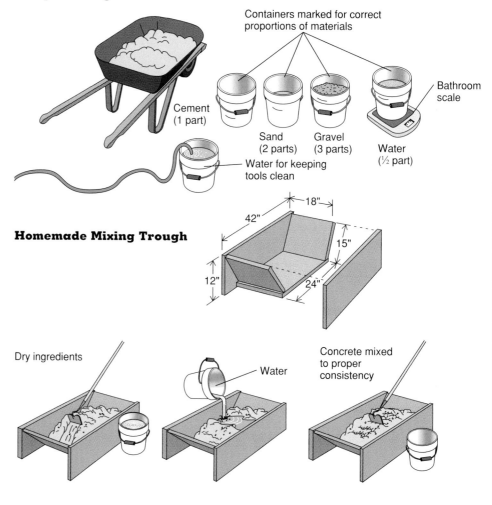

Cement (1 part)

Sand (2 parts)

Gravel (3 parts)

Water (½ part)

Containers marked for correct proportions of materials

Bathroom scale

Water for keeping tools clean

Homemade Mixing Trough

18"
42"
15"
12"
24"

Dry ingredients

Water

Concrete mixed to proper consistency

Decorative Piers

With most decks, the concrete piers are out of sight and out of mind, but if the under-structure of your deck will be in prominent view, you may want to give the piers some character. A simple way to give the exposed concrete sides of the piers an elegant texture is to make forming tubes out of 90-pound roll roofing material, with the mineral surface coating on the inside of the form. This technique gives the concrete a softened texture.

Another way to make piers more attractive is to build four-sided wood forms, then nail narrow triangular strips of wood into the four corners and along the top edges of the four sides. The hardened concrete will have beveled corners and top edges. You could also tack decorative shapes to the inside of the forms to create interesting voids in the fin-ished concrete; old numerals and alphabet letters from chil-dren's toy boxes create end-less possibilities. Finally, you can line the forms with bub-ble wrap or similar material to give the concrete surface an interesting texture.

Pouring Piers With Footings

Building Forms

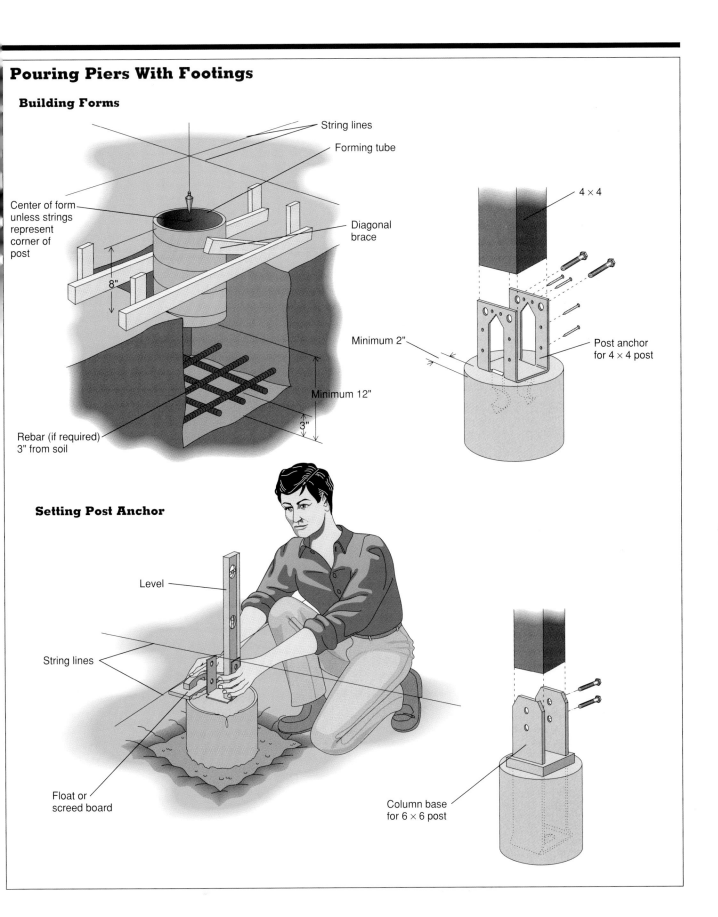

String lines

Forming tube

Center of form unless strings represent corner of post

Diagonal brace

8"

4 × 4

Minimum 2"

Minimum 12"

3"

Rebar (if required) 3" from soil

Post anchor for 4 × 4 post

Setting Post Anchor

Level

String lines

Float or screed board

Column base for 6 × 6 post

Mixing and Curing Concrete

The strength and durability of concrete are controlled by the proportions of dry ingredients and water. You can combine the dry ingredients yourself, purchase a prepared concrete mix, or order a delivery of ready-mixed concrete.

Using a Concrete Mix

A premix contains all of the dry ingredients—cement, sand, and gravel—in the proper ratio, allowing you to save the time needed to calculate, purchase, and combine the dry ingredients. It's easy to mix; all you do is add the right amount of water. Using concrete mix is fine for small jobs. The only drawback is the added expense for its convenience.

One 80-pound bag of concrete mix usually yields approximately ⅔ cubic foot (check bag label). To make one cubic yard, you would need to buy 40 sacks. You can mix one sack at a time in a garden wheelbarrow, two sacks in a contractor's wheelbarrow.

Combining Dry Ingredients

For relatively large jobs and to save money, you can mix the dry ingredients yourself. The formula is one part portland cement, two parts sand, and three parts gravel (1-inch diameter maximum) to five parts water. You can have the dry ingredients delivered, or haul them yourself. The chart below gives you an idea of the amount of cement, sand, gravel, and water you'll need to make various quantities of concrete.

Mixing Concrete

Mix concrete in a wheelbarrow, metal tub, homemade trough, or rented motorized mixer. Be sure to mix enough concrete in one batch to pour one entire footing and pier. If you don't, the first pour will begin to set up and, when the fresh batch is poured on top, "cold joints," which cause overall weakness and cracking, will form.

Be careful when mixing concrete. Follow all cautions printed on the bag. Try not to splash out any water, as this will alter the concrete's consistency. Follow the techniques below for hand mixing.

1. Use a separate container for each ingredient. For the first batch, place the container on a scale and add the ingredient until the proper weight is reached. Make a mark on the container to indicate the amount of that ingredient needed. Repeat for each container. For subsequent batches, just fill the containers to the marks.

2. Place the dry ingredients, in the proper ratio, or the cement mix in the mixing container. Mix thoroughly by digging down and pulling the material at the bottom over the top with a shovel or hoe. Pull from one end several times, then from the other end. (This does apply to concrete mix, since its ingredients may have settled in the bag.)

3. Form a depression in the middle of the dry mixture. Pour in part of the measured amount of water. Pull the dry mixture into the water until it is absorbed.

4. Add more water, a little at a time, and continue to mix. Don't add all the water at once; it makes mixing too difficult. With the shovel or hoe, make a series of hacks that leave ridges. Add more water if the ridges look dry and crumbly; add more dry ingredients in the proper ratio if the ridges look runny. Always add water or dry ingredients in very small increments.

Curing Concrete

To allow the concrete to cure properly, leave the forms in place for five to seven days. If you are pouring concrete during cold weather, you must protect it from freezing by covering it with insulation. Once the concrete is completely cured, continue with installing the deck posts.

---

bottom will be 12 inches (or the thickness of the footing) above the bottom of the hole.

Position the cut section of the tube between two 1 by 3s (or scrap lumber) cut long enough to bridge across the hole. The bottom edges of the boards should be 8 inches below the top of the tube (12 inches if the site is sloped). Nail the tube to each board with a 1-inch roofing nail from inside the tube, or with an 8d duplex nail through the boards into the tube, angling it upward.

Restring the layout lines and, with a plumb bob and measuring tape, position each tube so it is centered exactly where its post will be centered. Then nail one end of a short 1 by 2 (or scrap of lumber) to the top edge of the tube and, with a torpedo level, adjust the tube so it is plumb (perfectly vertical); then nail the bottom of the 1 by 2 to one of the supporting boards, to create a diagonal brace that holds the tube plumb. Secure the ends of the supporting boards with stakes driven into

Proportions of Ingredients for Making Concrete

	Cubic Feet of Concrete				
	4	6	12	18	27*
Cement (90-lb sacks)	1	1½	3	4½	6
Sand (pounds)	200	300	600	900	1,400
Gravel (pounds)	300	450	900	1,350	2,025
Water (gallons)	5	7½	15	22½	33¾
or Water (pounds)	40	60	120	180	270

*1 cubic yard

Pouring Footings for Precast Piers

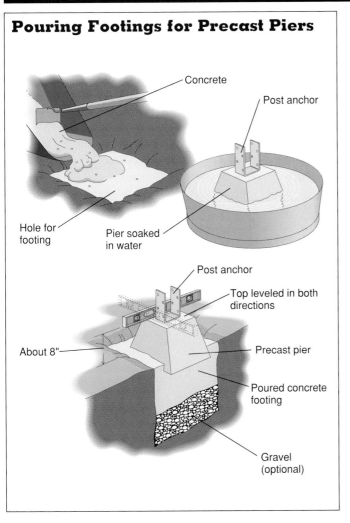

Concrete

Post anchor

Hole for footing

Pier soaked in water

Post anchor

Top leveled in both directions

About 8"

Precast pier

Poured concrete footing

Gravel (optional)

the ground or with weights, such as bricks or concrete blocks. Cut one or two pieces of ½-inch (No. 4) rebar 6 to 8 inches longer than the tube and set them beside the hole so they will be handy for placing in the wet concrete.

Finally, remove the string lines and call for an inspection, if required. Note: If rebar is required in the footing, wire together a grid with three or four bars crossing in each direction and set it in the bottom of the hole on 3-inch "dobies" (square concrete blocks). No steel should be within 3 inches of the soil.

To pour each footing, first remove loose dirt from the bottom of the footing hole, or tamp it solid with a 2 by 4. Place about 6 inches of gravel in the bottom of the hole and tamp it. Mix enough concrete for only one footing and pier. Place enough concrete in the hole to fill it slightly higher than the bottom of the tube, then consolidate the concrete by jabbing a piece of rebar or other rod up and down in it. Then fill the pier form, consolidating the concrete by using a rod and by tapping the side of the form with a hammer. Strike off, or level,

the concrete at the top of the pier with a scrap of wood or a wooden float. Wait a few minutes for the concrete to set up, then insert the reinforcing bars vertically into the center of the pier until the top ends are 1 inch below the surface of the concrete.

Next, while the concrete is still fresh, restring the layout lines. Using the layout lines, a plumb bob, and a tape measure, ascertain the position for a metal post anchor and embed it in the top of each pier. (Be sure to orient all brackets in the same direction.) Place a level on all sides of the anchor to check for plumb, being careful not to disturb the concrete. Carefully adjust the anchor as needed, jiggling it slightly so the concrete will consolidate around the embedded flanges. Repeat the process for each footing and pier.

For safety, mark each bracket with a bright ribbon or other warning, or cover it with an inverted box, barrel, or bucket. If necessary, fence off the site to prevent someone from tripping over the brackets and getting injured.

For maximum strength, leave the pier forms in place and undisturbed for at least five days, so the concrete will cure fully. Moisture is needed for hydration, the chemical process by which cement mixed with water hardens; removing the forms too soon allows moisture to evaporate.

Pouring Footings for Use With Precast Piers

There are several styles of precast piers available, but for most deck posts the type with a metal post anchor built into it is best. In a few situations—for instance, where a low profile or quick connections are required—other types may be more suitable.

Excavate the footing holes to the required depth, allowing for an additional 6 inches of gravel. To set a pier, first place the gravel in the bottom of the footing hole and tamp it firm. Mix only enough concrete for one footing and pour it into the hole, then smooth and level the top of the footing just below grade with a scrap of 2 by 4. Wait a few minutes, or until the concrete begins to set up.

In the meantime, soak the precast pier with water from a garden hose or in a bucket. Restring the layout lines and, using a plumb bob and tape measure, position the pier over the footing so the post anchor will be centered on the footing. Take into consideration the direction in which you want the bolts and brackets to align; they should all be turned in the same direction. Push the pier slightly into the footing, so that the top is at least 8 inches above grade, and check that it is level in all directions. Repeat the process for each footing and pier. Give the concrete five days to cure properly before continuing with the post installation.

FRAMING THE DECK

The framework that supports the decking consists of posts, beams, joists, and related blocking or bracing. The sequence and techniques that are described on the following pages assume a one-directional decking pattern parallel with the house wall; if you plan to install decking in a decorative pattern, see page 65 for alternate joist layouts.

Step 6: Install the Posts

This is one of those tasks where the rule of thumb to "measure twice, cut once" certainly applies. It also takes two people, so line up an assistant before you begin.

Refer to your plans to determine the height of the posts in relation to the beams and ledger board. Cut the posts approximately 6 to 12 inches longer than needed. If your deck design calls for extended posts that reach up to the railing, don't cut the posts. Just mark them for placement of the beams.

Start with one of the outermost posts, and have an assistant hold it in position in the post anchor. Check for plumb on two adjacent sides with a carpenter's level. Make a mark on the post level with the top of the ledger board. There are several ways to do this: with a layout string line, if the lines are level; with a line level suspended from a string; with a hydro level; with a builder's level; or with a long straightedge with a carpenter's level placed on it. The mark on the post indicates the height of the post, plus the beam depth, plus the joist depth, plus clearance for any hardware that will come between the top of the post and the beam.

Take down the post. From the line marked on the post, subtract the total of the beam depth, joist depth, and hardware clearance. Mark this point on all four sides of the post. Assuming that the post will not extend all the way to the railing, cut it to length. If it will extend to the railing, wait to trim it to the exact length until after the deck structure is built and the decking is installed. Dip all sawed ends into a clear wood preservative. If the top of the post will be difficult to reach after it's erected, attach the beam-connecting hardware to the post now. Note: If your plans call for a header board or

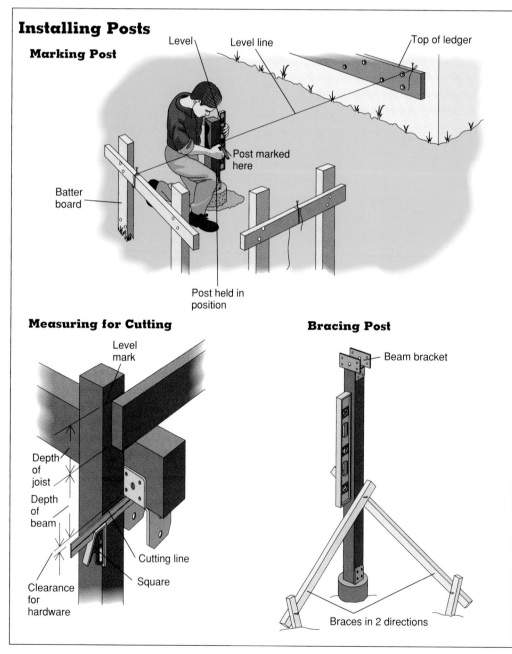

Installing Posts

Marking Post

Level — Level line — Top of ledger — Post marked here — Batter board — Post held in position

Measuring for Cutting

Level mark — Depth of joist — Depth of beam — Cutting line — Square — Clearance for hardware

Bracing Post

Beam bracket — Braces in 2 directions

beam bolted to the sides of the posts instead of attached to the top, or if joists will be attached to the beam with hangers instead of resting on top of it, alter the dimensions accordingly.

Fasten the post securely to the post anchor with screws, bolts, or nails, then add temporary bracing made of scrap lumber nailed to two adjacent sides of the post and fixed to a stake in the ground. The bracing keeps the post secure and plumb until the beams are installed.

Next, measure, cut, and erect the post on the adjacent corner. To mark the cutting lines of any posts positioned between these corner posts, simply stretch a chalk line between them and snap it against the other posts.

For a stand-alone deck, measure the post height according to the deck plan, subtracting the thickness of the beam, joists, and hardware, as necessary. Cut one post to length, install it, and add the temporary bracing. Measure all of the other posts from this post, using a line level, builder's level, hydro level, or long straightedge and carpenter's level to mark the proper height.

Step 7: Install the Beams

The beams carry the weight of the joists, decking, accessories, and people, and transfer it to the posts. When you are working with the beams, be sure the crown, where the grain curves, faces up. This way, the weight of the deck straightens it out.

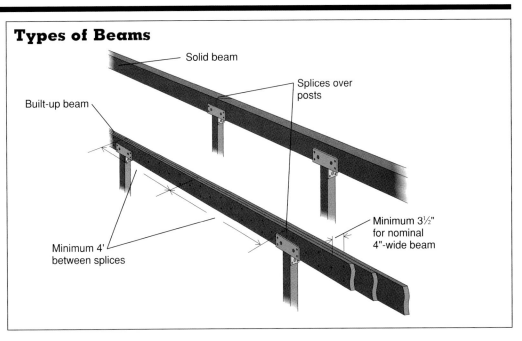

Types of Beams

Solid beam

Splices over posts

Built-up beam

Minimum 4' between splices

Minimum 3½" for nominal 4"-wide beam

Solid Versus Built-up

Because beams are major load-bearing components of the deck, they must be sized carefully. Generally, solid lumber (such as 4-by or 6-by lumber) should be your first choice, because it will shorten your construction time considerably, and because a solid piece of lumber won't collect rot-causing moisture or debris, as built-up beams can.

However, solid lumber in long lengths is costly, and you may not find it readily available. Also consider that its weight makes it slightly more difficult to handle if you are moving lumber by hand to a remote deck location.

In sizing built-up, or laminated, beams, note that two 2-bys nailed together do not create a 4-by beam, and they cannot span the same distance. Two 2 by 10s, for example, do not make a 4 by 10, because their combined thickness is only 3 inches (1½ inches + 1½

inches), not the 3½-inch width of a 4 by 10. To bridge a span requiring a 4 by 10, use three 2 by 10s nailed together.

Making Built-up Beams

To make built-up beams, select the size lumber you will need in lengths you feel comfortable handling. Always use pressure-treated lumber. To construct the beams, first plan where any end splices will fall. It's important that end-to-end splices of outside members be located over posts, not in midspan. Splices should also be spaced so that none is within 4 feet of any others.

Cut each board square and to length, and apply preservative to the cut ends. Lay the pieces in position and fasten them together, face-to-face, with galvanized bolts, lag screws, or 12d nails, spaced about 3 inches apart and staggered top and bottom. For added strength, reinforce all outside splices with post caps, metal fastener straps, or cleats.

The lumber may be crooked; in order to keep the pieces in straight alignment as you nail or bolt them together, stretch a string along one edge of the bottom piece to check for straightness.

Attaching Beams to Posts

The easiest and strongest way to attach beams to posts is with metal post caps or column caps. Be sure to buy the proper size—the nominal size is usually for surfaced lumber; unsurfaced (full-cut) lumber or built-up beams require different sizes of brackets. Alternative methods of connecting the beams to the posts are bolting T-straps or wood cleats to the sides of the connection, or sandwiching a built-up post between the outer members of a built-up beam. Whichever method you choose, be sure to install the beam with its crown facing up so the weight of the deck will straighten the bow.

57

Connecting Beam to Post

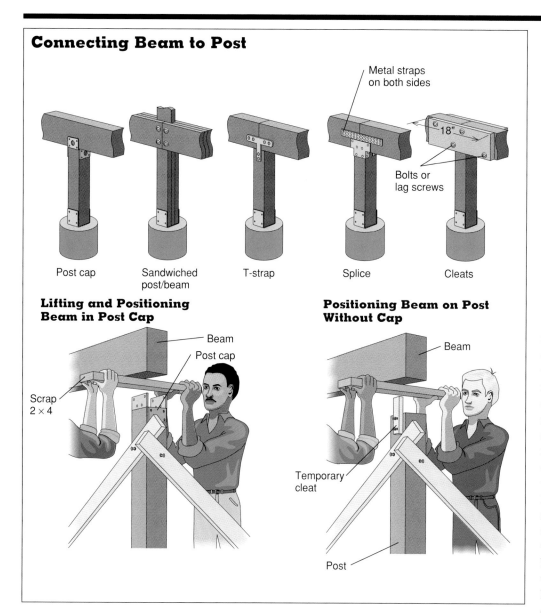

Metal straps on both sides

18"

Bolts or lag screws

Post cap   Sandwiched post/beam   T-strap   Splice   Cleats

Lifting and Positioning Beam in Post Cap

Beam
Post cap
Scrap 2 × 4

Positioning Beam on Post Without Cap

Beam
Temporary cleat
Post

If you're not using post caps or similar metal connectors, you will need a temporary guide to help position the beams on top of the posts. Nail a cleat on one side of each post so it extends a few inches above the top of the post. This guide will act as a backstop when you line up and place the beams.

Before installing a beam, cut it to the exact length. A splice, or joint, should be centered over the top of a post.

If the ends of a beam will be exposed, give them a more finished appearance by shaping them. A simple technique is to chamfer the bottom edges (cut them off at a 45-degree angle). You could also round the edges with a saber saw and some sanding. If you feel especially creative, you might try carving a whale head, giant thumb, gargoyle, or other whimsical shape.

Get help installing the beams. Don't attempt to lift them by yourself. Relatively lightweight beams can be easily lifted, positioned, and secured by two people, but heavier beams definitely call for more helpers.

Here's a simple technique for easy and safe lifting. Select a beam and move it to the installation location. Place a short length (2 to 3 feet) of 2 by 4 lumber under one end of the beam and at right angles to

it. With a helper, use the 2 by 4 to lift that end and place it on top of the post. Drive one nail through the post cap or connector, or the temporary guide, and into the beam. Lift and secure the other end of the beam in the same way. Check the level and plumb of the beam and posts, and make adjustments to the beam's placement as necessary.

Remove the nail from the connector or guide and permanently attach the beam to the posts with carriage bolts or machine bolts. Drill holes through the beams and posts for each bolt, using a bit ⅛ inch larger than the diameter of the bolt. Depending on the thickness of the lumber, you may need an extralong drill bit or shaft extension, or you may need to drill from both sides. Use the holes in the metal brackets as guides. After drilling, run the bolts through the holes and secure the beam. If a bolt won't go through a hole because drilling from opposite sides of the beam was not in perfect alignment, bend the bolt slightly by whacking it with a sledgehammer. Nails or lag screws can also be used to fasten the beams to the posts.

Step 8: Install Permanent Bracing

Bracing requirements are specified by local building codes. Typically, decks with posts higher than 5 feet and decks that may be subjected to high winds, earthquakes, tremors, or shifting soil must be braced, but all decks benefit from some permanent bracing.

Bracing Posts

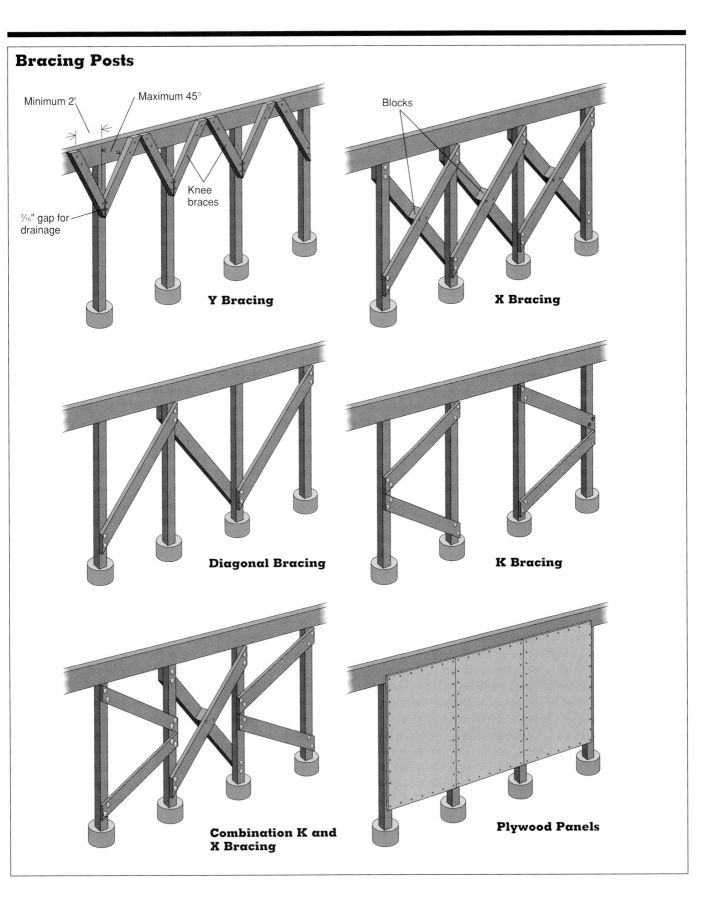

Minimum 2'

Maximum 45°

Knee braces

³⁄₁₆" gap for drainage

Y Bracing

Blocks

X Bracing

Diagonal Bracing

K Bracing

Combination K and X Bracing

Plywood Panels

59

Permanent bracing can be attached to just the posts or to the posts and beams. Use 2 by 4s for bracing distances that are less than 8 feet; use 2 by 6s for longer distances. Attach the bracing with carriage bolts or lag screws. Where the ends of the braces butt together, leave a little space so the joint won't trap water.

Step 9: Install the Joists

Joists, which distribute the weight of the decking boards evenly over the beams and ledger, are cut from 2-by lumber. The joist size (width) is determined by the joist span (distance between beams or ledger and beam), the joist spacing (distance between joist centers), and the species and grade of lumber used.

Laying Out the Joists

To mark the joist positions on the ledger and the beams, use a pencil, a combination square, and a tape measure or story board (a long scrap of lumber used for a measuring template).

First, locate and mark the positions of the two outside joists on the ledger board. Place an X on the side of each mark where the joist itself goes, so there will be no confusion about whether a mark refers to the inside or outside edge of a joist. Refer to your deck plans for the spacing of the remaining joists, then measure and mark their positions on the board. Draw a vertical line through each mark, using a combination square or a

level to keep it straight and plumb. Remember that the joist spacing does not refer to the distance between joists, but to the distance between the joist centers (or left edges or right edges).

If your tape measure does not have 16-inch increments highlighted (16-, 32-, 48-, 64-, 80-inch marks, and so on), here's an easy way to transfer these marks to each beam. Lay a story board on top of the ledger board and, with a combination square, transfer the joist marks from the ledger board to the face of the story board. Then, using the layout string lines to align the end of the story board, lay the board on the beam and transfer the marks on the story board to the beam. Using a combination square, draw a line at each mark across the top of the beam; place an X next to the line to mark the side on which the joist will go.

If you will be lapping joists over a beam because they are not long enough to span the entire width of the deck, allow for the "jog" when marking the joist positions—the joist layout on one side of the beam will be offset 1½ inches from the joist layout on the other side (see opposite page).

Cutting the Joists

Joist lumber should be properly dried and straight, and should have few imperfections, such as loose knots. "Sight" each piece carefully and determine the crown (the edge that bows upward at the middle), then mark the joist with an arrow so the crown will be facing up when

the joist is installed. If the joists will rest on top of the beams, wait to trim the outside ends of the joists until after you install them. If you are installing the joists by attaching both ends to the ledger and/or beams with joist hangers, measure the joist spans between the beams, allow for ⅛-inch clearance at each end of each joist, and cut all the joists before installing them. Using metal joist hangers allows as much as ½-inch discrepancy between joist lengths, so if the distance between beams does not vary more than that, you can cut all the joists to the same length. If

there is greater variation, measure and cut each joist individually. Apply preservative to the cut ends.

When Joists Are Too Short

If joist lumber is not available in the lengths you need, you will need to join the shorter pieces of lumber by splicing them or by lapping them over a beam. Laps should extend 6 to 12 inches beyond each side of the beam. The overlap method is easier, but remember to allow for the jog when marking the joist positions on the ledger board or beam.

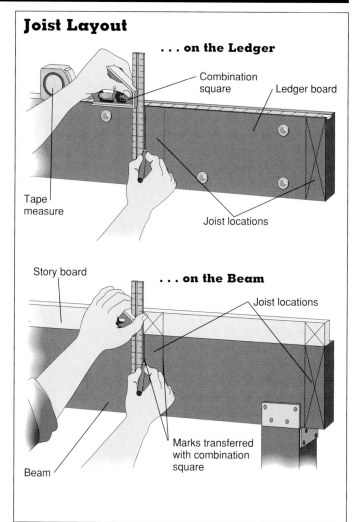

Joist Layout

. . . on the Ledger

Combination square
Ledger board
Tape measure
Joist locations

Story board
. . . on the Beam
Joist locations
Marks transferred with combination square
Beam

Measuring for Joist Length

Joists Recessed Between Beams

Joists Resting on Beam

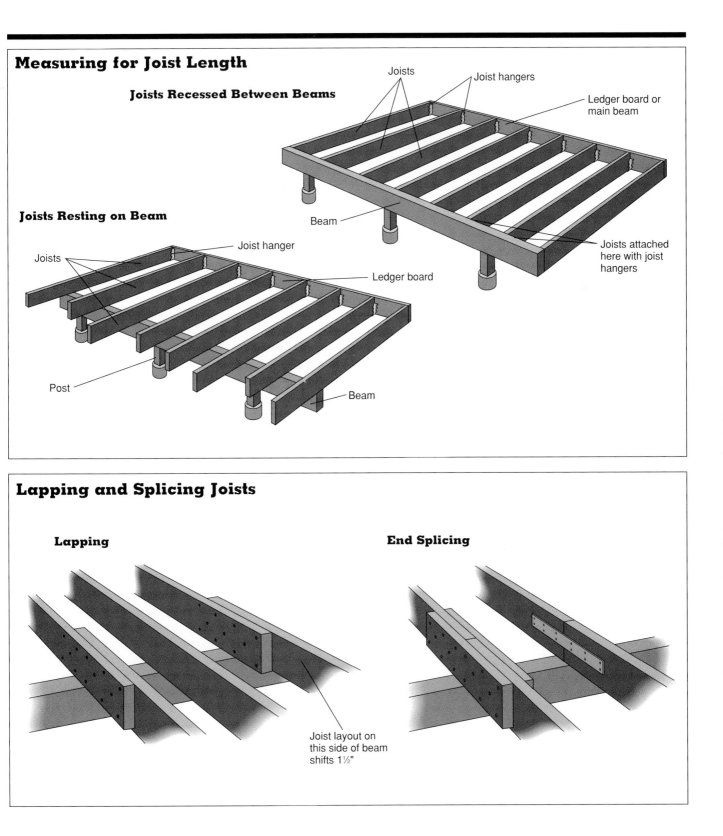

Joists

Joist hangers

Ledger board or main beam

Joist hanger

Joists

Beam

Ledger board

Joists attached here with joist hangers

Post

Beam

Lapping and Splicing Joists

Lapping

End Splicing

Joist layout on this side of beam shifts 1½"

There are two ways to splice a joist: with a metal strap, or by sandwiching the ends between short (18 to 24 inches) pieces of joist lumber. Sandwiching provides greater strength.

There are two rules for placing overlaps and splices. First, stagger their placement; don't position the splice or overlap at the same location on each joist. Second, place the splice or lap over a beam. This will require a little planning as you measure and cut.

Installing the Joists

Before installing any joists, attach the joist hangers to the ledger board, on the Xs. To position each hanger at the right height, insert a scrap piece of joist lumber in it and align the top edge of the scrap with the top of the ledger board. Nail only one side of each hanger into position, using galvanized joist-hanger nails. If the joists will be attached to the facing beam with joist hangers, attach hangers to the beam in the same manner.

Install the two outside joists first. If you are attaching them to the ends of the ledger board, rather than hanging them with joist hangers, drill two pilot holes through the end of each joist. Nail each joist to the ledger board with three 16d galvanized spiral-shank nails, then strengthen the corner with an angle bracket nailed on the inside with galvanized joist-hanger nails. Secure the other end of the joist to the facing beam in the same manner, if the

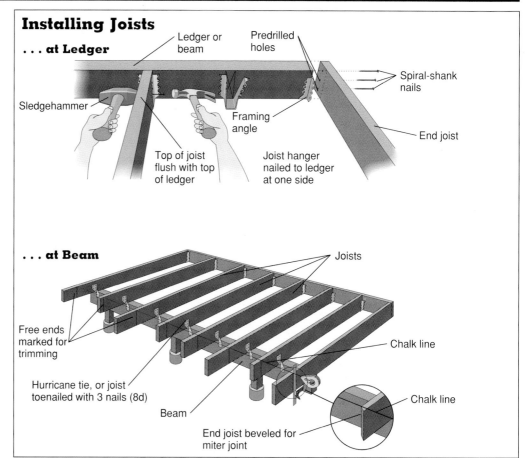

Installing Joists

. . . at Ledger

Ledger or beam — Predrilled holes — Spiral-shank nails — Sledgehammer — Framing angle — End joist — Top of joist flush with top of ledger — Joist hanger nailed to ledger at one side

. . . at Beam

Joists — Free ends marked for trimming — Hurricane tie, or joist toenailed with 3 nails (8d) — Beam — Chalk line — Chalk line — End joist beveled for miter joint

beam is the same height as the ledger, or by resting the joist on top of the beam and toenailing it with three 8d galvanized common nails.

Install each inside joist, one at a time, by sliding the end into the hanger so there is at least ⅛-inch clearance at the end. Squeeze the unattached side of the joist hanger closed and nail it to the ledger board. Then nail the hanger to the joist; when nailing the second side, hold a sledgehammer against the hanger on the opposite side to prevent nails from coming loose. Attach the other end of the joist before installing the next joist. If the joist rests on top of the facing beam, toenail it to the beam with three 8d galvanized com-

mon nails, or with a metal hurricane tie attached to the face of the beam and the side of the joist.

Installing the Joist Header

If the joists extend beyond the outside beam (are cantilevered), you must stabilize the open joist ends by covering them with a joist header. Do this the same day the joists are installed, or their ends may warp. First, trim the joists to length. To do this, measure and mark the required width of the deck along each of the two outside joists. Subtract 1½ inches from these marks (the thickness of the header) and snap a chalk line between the new marks across the tops of

the joists. With a square, transfer the chalk mark to the face of each joist. Cut them with a power circular saw, and apply wood preservative to the joist ends. Cut the joist header to length. Predrill both ends of the header to prevent nails from splitting them. Start at one end of the header and, with a helper holding the other end, attach the header to each joist with three 16d galvanized box or spiral-shank nails, or galvanized deck screws. Note: If you want to make miter joints at the corners, leave the two outside joists 1½ inches longer than the inside joists and cut 45-degree bevels on the ends of the header joist and the outside joists.

Joist Blocking and Bridging

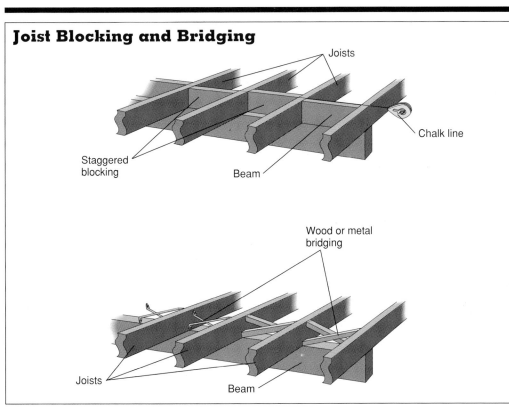

Joists

Staggered blocking

Beam

Chalk line

Wood or metal bridging

Joists

Beam

Stabilizing the Joists

Bracing between the joists adds strength and rigidity to the entire deck structure. It prevents joists from rolling over, twisting, and flexing, and stops those noticeable squeaks and creaks when you walk on the deck's surface. There are two methods of bracing joists: blocking and bridging. Blocking, which is the easiest method, uses short pieces of joist lumber that fit snugly between the joists. Bridging is more difficult and is not used very often on decks. It consists of two pieces that crisscross between the joists; if you use wood bridging, you must cut the ends at precise angles. You might want to look for galvanized metal bridging at your home-improvement center. It is sold for specific joist spacings.

Generally, blocking or bridging is required between joists wherever they rest on beams and at least every 8 feet along spans, but be sure to check your local building code for the required spacing.

To lay out the blocking or bridging, start at the outermost beam. For blocking over beams, locate the centerline of the beam and mark it on top of the two outside joists. Snap a chalk line across the rest of the joists between the two marks. Then, using a combination or framing square, transfer the chalk mark onto the face of each joist. Mark other rows of blocking, if required, at the middle of joist spans, unless the midpoint is more than 8 feet from the nearest row of blocking. Note: To prevent moisture from being trapped between the

blocking and the beam, adjust the marks so the blocking will be positioned slightly off the beam instead of directly on it.

Blocking

Cut blocking from the same 2-by lumber as the joists. To determine the length of each block, measure the distance between the joists along the chalk line. Theoretically, all these distances are equal, but they usually vary slightly, so measure for every block. The blocking must fit snugly, without bowing the joists.

You can make nailing easier by alternating blocks on either side of the centerline. If you prefer the appearance of straight-line blocking, you will have to toenail one end of each block. Nail each end with three 16d galvanized common or spiral-shank nails.

As you progress along a line of blocking, sight along a few joists to see if any are being pushed out of alignment. If so, trim the next block to keep the next joist in line. When you have finished installing the blocking, recheck all the connections. Some of the blocks may have worked their way loose while you were nailing farther along the beam. Tighten them up by tapping a sledgehammer against the whole line of blocking until it is snug.

Bridging

The bridging method requires measuring from the top edge of one joist to the bottom edge of its facing joist. The ends of the bridging pieces, usually made from 2 by 4s, are cut at an angle, which is determined by the distance between the joists and the width of the joist lumber. Cut one bridging piece to the correct length, making sure the ends are cut to the correct angle. If you find that the joist spacing is exactly the same, use this first piece as a pattern to cut all the rest. If the spacing varies, however, you must cut the pieces separately for each joist space. Place each piece against the centerline, alternating pieces on either side of it. Fasten each end with galvanized 8d common nails or 2-inch galvanized deck screws.

When you have completed installing the bridging pieces, recheck them and, if necessary, tighten each connection. Some of the pieces may have worked themselves loose as you nailed farther along.

DECKING BOARDS

The decking is a dominant element of any deck, and small details make a difference in the overall appearance. Because deck boards are easy and enjoyable to install, you should find it a pleasant challenge to work carefully as you select, place, and fasten each board.

Step 10: Install the Decking

Before you lay the decking, complete any remaining work on the deck's substructure. If you plan to apply a protective finish to the substructure or install plumbing or wiring, do it now while you have easy access. To increase the longevity of the deck, install sealing strips along the top of each joist to prevent moisture from penetrating into the joists along the decking nails.

The most common sizes for decking boards are 2 by 4 and 2 by 6. Along with the newer ¾-inch by 6-inch size, these are also the most desirable. Anything smaller or larger tends to sag, warp, twist, or cup. The exact size of decking material you should use is dictated by the joist spans and by the pattern you select for your decking. Most decks are built with 2 by 6 or ¾-inch by 6-inch lumber.

Laying Out the Boards

Before fastening any boards, lay out all but the last few boards on the joists. This allows you to arrange them for the best appearance, and creates a working platform. (*Warning:* Be extremely cautious where boards butt together at a joist, or overhang the outside edges of the deck!) Leave a space about 4 inches wide at the beginning of your layout, along the house wall, so you will have room to maneuver boards as you move them into place for fastening.

Ideally, you should use decking lumber that is just a little longer than the width of the deck, but this may be impossible because of availability, cost, or deck design. If it's necessary to butt decking boards together, plan to position the joints over joists, and stagger them.

When measuring and cutting the decking, let the boards hang over the edges of the outside joists, then trim off the ends after all the decking has been installed. Since the decking is exposed to the elements, you should give it extra protection by coating it with wood preservative after you cut it to size. Be sure to soak the edges and ends with the preservative. The second coat should cover the entire deck and should be applied when the deck is finished.

Position the boards so the "bark side" is up (the half circles of the end-grain pattern resemble a rainbow) to minimize grain separation and splitting on the top of the boards. Also, for a more uniform look, position all the boards so their top grain runs in the same direction. Select knot-free boards to go in front of the doorways, picture windows, stairs, and other entrances to the deck.

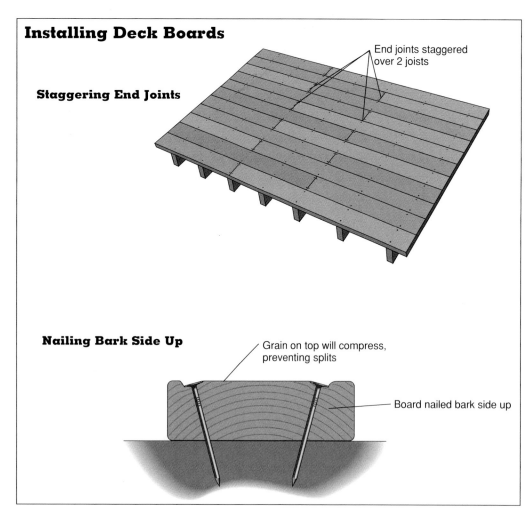

Installing Deck Boards

Staggering End Joints

End joints staggered over 2 joists

Nailing Bark Side Up

Grain on top will compress, preventing splits

Board nailed bark side up

Selecting a Decking Pattern

You can create a special character for your deck with the decking pattern. A simple arrangement is usually the best choice; complex patterns tend to accentuate rather than hide any defects in the decking. And, as the illustrations show, even the simplest pattern can add special interest and dimension to your deck. For an unusual effect, you can arrange 2 by 4s and 2 by 6s in repeated sequences.

For a clean, finished look, add borders with mitered corners to the perimeter of the deck after decking is installed.

Whatever design you choose, plan its layout carefully, giving special consideration to the location of joints. This will give the deck a uniform look.

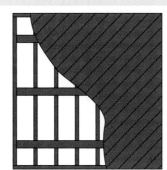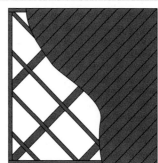

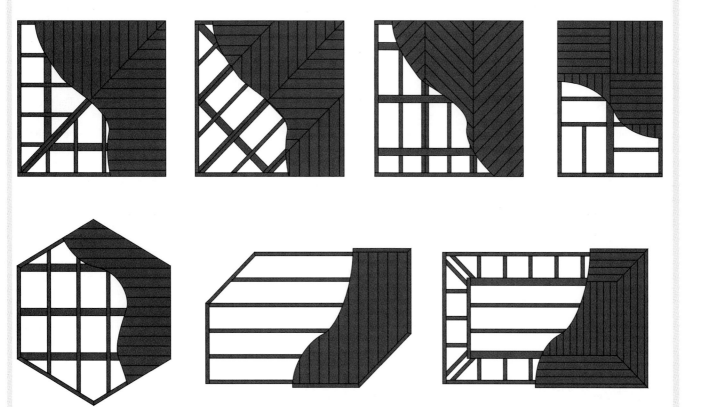

Alternative Fasteners

Screws

Although they're more expensive than nails, galvanized decking screws are stronger, and make it easy to remove boards. Buy screws that are long enough to penetrate the joists to a depth at least equal to the thickness of the decking boards. You can fasten them with a power screwdriver. Set the clutch adjustment so the screw heads are countersunk slightly below the surface of the boards. Some power screwdrivers have automatic screw-feeding clips.

Decking Clips

Decking clips are expensive, but if you prefer a deck surface that is smooth and nail-free, the clips are worth the expense. They also last longer than nails or screws. To use decking clips, you start by toenailing the first decking board in place, then use the clips starting with the second board. Mount the clips on the edge of the board that will face the first board, securing one clip about 2 inches from each joist location. Install the decking by sliding the clip's prong under the first decking board, then toenail the opposite edge to the joists. Repeat this process to install the rest of the decking.

Decking Adhesive

The advantages of an adhesive are a nail-free deck surface, faster installation time, and a longer-lasting deck surface. However, adhesive does not work well if decking boards are crooked and need to be straightened. Apply the adhesive to the top of the joists with a caulking gun, then set the decking boards in place. Once the adhesive has set up, it will be nearly impossible for you to remove the boards without damaging them and the joists below. This could be a problem if you need to make repairs or access the area underneath in the future.

Continuous-Strip Fasteners

This deck-fastening system, which is relatively new, consists of galvanized metal strips that lie on the top edges of the joists. Each strip has a flange with predrilled holes for nailing it to the side of the joist. The deck boards are laid over the top of the strips, then fastened from below with screws driven up through predrilled holes in the metal strip. No fasteners are visible on top of the decking, and no fasteners penetrate the tops of the joists.

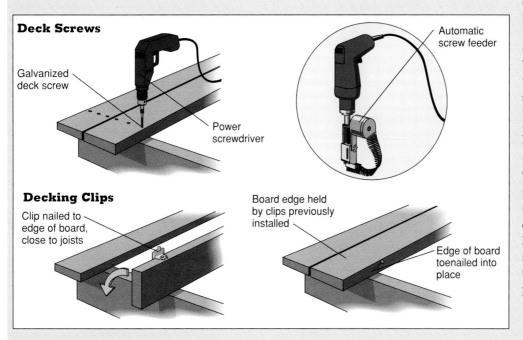

Deck Screws
- Galvanized deck screw
- Power screwdriver
- Automatic screw feeder

Decking Clips
- Clip nailed to edge of board, close to joists
- Board edge held by clips previously installed
- Edge of board toenailed into place

Fastening the Decking

You can fasten the decking to the joists with nails, screws, deck clips, decking adhesive, or continuous-strip fasteners. Regardless of the method you choose, you may want to use screws for boards in the area above any plumbing or electrical lines. This way, the deck boards can be easily removed for maintenance and repairs.

Start installing the decking with the first board along the house wall. Cut the board to the exact length, so you won't need to cut close to the siding when you cut the other boards to length later. Be sure the board is perfectly straight, and leave a ¼-inch gap along the siding so water won't be trapped. If you're working on a stand-alone deck, start at the most prominent side.

As you fasten the decking to each joist, allow a ¹⁄₁₆- to ³⁄₁₆-inch gap between the boards for drainage, ventilation, expansion, and contraction. To keep the gap consistent across the deck, make a guide with a 10d nail driven through the center of a strip of scrap wood. As you install the decking, use the nail to create the crack between the boards, snugging the new board up to it (the wood scrap will keep the nail from falling through the cracks).

Nailing Tips

Nailing is the simplest, least expensive way to fasten the decking to the joists. Hand-nailing is better than power nailers; even though nailers will fasten the decking much more quickly, they shoot nails too far into the decking and the nails are more likely to rise up over time. Here are some helpful tips for nailing the decking to the joists.

1. You must use nails long enough to penetrate the joists to a depth equal to the thickness of the decking. If your decking is 1½ inches thick, the nail should penetrate the joist at least 1½ inches.

2. Depending on the width of the decking, use two or three nails to attach the decking at each joist. Keep the nails in straight lines across the decking so the nail heads have a clean appearance. Use a framing square as a nailing guide, aligning it with nails in the previous two boards as you place nails for each joist.

3. Nails driven straight down through the decking can split the decking or soon work their way out. Drive the nails into the decking at about 30° opposing angles.

4. To avoid splitting, especially at the ends of the decking, use this carpenter's trick: Before starting a nail, blunt the tip slightly by tapping it with your hammer or on the head of a nail already driven into a board. Nails with blunted points drill their own holes as they penetrate the wood. If the decking still splits, especially at the ends of boards, drill pilot holes with a power drill. Here's another trick: Nail only into the light part of the grain pattern, not directly on the dark grain lines where the wood is more brittle.

5. When pulling nails, place a wood block under the hammer head for better leverage, to keep from breaking the handle, and to protect the surface of the decking boards. Pull the handle back toward you with a curved-claw hammer and side to side with a framing hammer with a ripping claw.

6. As you drive each nail, be careful not to damage the surface of the decking by missing the nail head, because the hammer head may create indentations where water can collect. This can also happen if you try to drive the nail in too far with a hammer. Always drive the nails in until they rest ¹⁄₁₆ to ⅛ inch above the surface, then use a nail set to drive them below the surface of the board.

7. If you accidentally dent the decking with the hammer, treat the area with a small amount of warm water, which will cause the wood to swell back to its normal size.

8. As the decking weathers, some nails will rise slightly. When the deck is one to two months old, reset the nail heads just below the surface with a hammer and nail set.

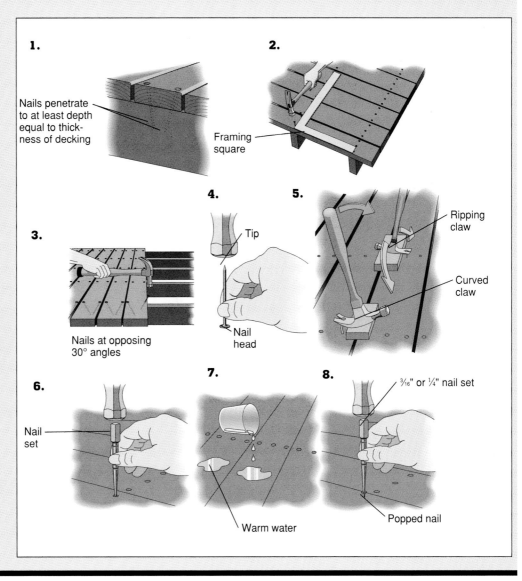

1.
Nails penetrate to at least depth equal to thickness of decking

2.
Framing square

3.
Nails at opposing 30° angles

4.
Tip
Nail head

5.
Ripping claw
Curved claw

6.
Nail set

7.
Warm water

8.
³⁄₁₆" or ¼" nail set
Popped nail

Straightening Bowed Boards

As you fasten the decking, you may come across a few boards that are bowed. This is a problem you can correct with a little know-how. First, use one nail at each end of the decking to secure it to the end joists. If the decking bows toward the last board you fastened, carefully force a chisel between the two boards and pry the bowed board outward, then nail it in place. If the bow curves away from the last board, drive the chisel into the joist on the outside of the curve and push on it to force the board into place, and nail it.

Notching for Posts

If you need to fit decking boards around extended posts, cut notches in the decking boards. Lay a piece of decking in position beside the post. On the board, mark the width of the post plus ⅜ inch for drainage. This is the width of the notch. To determine the depth, push the board tightly against the post, then measure how much the board must slide forward to fit neatly into place. If it is the last board of the layout, this dimension will be the distance from the board's edge to the outside edge of the header joist, plus ½-inch allowance for an overhang.

Using a combination square, draw the outline of the notch on the board. Then cut the two sides of the notch carefully with a circular saw or handsaw, keeping the blade on the inside of each line. Use a chisel to cut along the third line and remove the waste piece. If the wood grain is not straight and parallel with the cutting line, don't try to remove the waste with one bite of the chisel; instead, nibble it away with a series of smaller bites, starting from the edge.

Straightening Bowed Boards

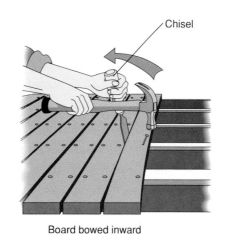

Chisel

Board bowed inward

Chisel

Board bowed outward

Notching for Post

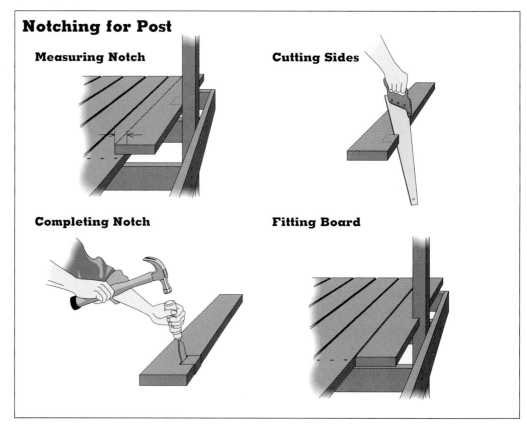

Measuring Notch

Cutting Sides

Completing Notch

Fitting Board

Trimming the Ends

After all of the decking is installed, trim off the overhanging ends. Marking and trimming the decking all at once saves time and makes a uniform, straight edge. Simply snap a chalk line carefully along the edge of the deck; if necessary, add an allowance for such features as fascia or trim boards to cover the joists, or a ½-inch overhang to create a shadow line. Use a circular saw to cut along the line. For a perfectly straight line, tack a board onto the decking to serve as a guide for the saw. Use a sharp blade to minimize splintering. Smooth the cut edges with a rasping plane or sander.

Adding a Fascia Board

Unless the joist header is an attractive piece of knot-free lumber, or you plan to paint the deck, you may want to install a decorative fascia board to give the edge of the deck a trim appearance. To do so, select long, straight, clear pieces of 2-by lumber. Some lumberyards sell a grade of lumber called fascia texture, which is smooth on one side and rough-sawed on the other, depending on the texture you prefer. Attach fascia boards to the deck after you install the stairs (the next task) but before you install the railing. Use miter joints at the corners. If one board is not long enough to span the entire length of the deck, making it necessary to splice two pieces end to end, cut the end of each piece at a 45-degree bevel so the ends will overlap at the joint. To prevent nail heads from marring the surface, attach the fascia boards with galvanized deck screws driven through the joists (or joist header) into the fascia board from behind.

Trimming Ends

Chalk line

Fascia boards give a clean, finished look to these steps and deck.

STAIRS AND RAILINGS

Deck stairs and railings must be designed and built carefully. They affect the accessibility and usability of the deck, they have a strong visual impact, and their design is governed by strict safety considerations.

Typical Stair Dimensions

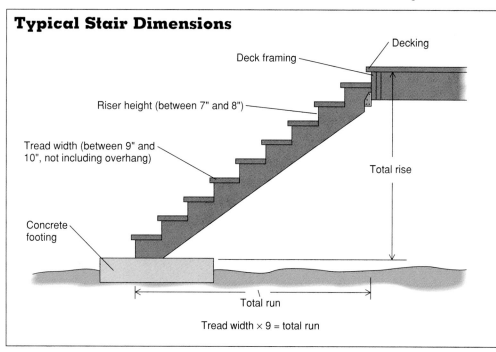

Decking

Deck framing

Riser height (between 7" and 8")

Tread width (between 9" and 10", not including overhang)

Total rise

Concrete footing

Total run

Tread width × 9 = total run

Within the strict code requirements for railings and stairs, there is still room for beauty, drama, and individuality.

Step 11: Build the Stairs

Although some low decks may need only a stepping-stone, most decks require at least one flight of stairs. If the deck has more than one stairway, the riser and tread dimensions should be consistent throughout all the flights. Your plans will probably specify the stair dimensions, but you should always calculate exact dimensions from site measurements, not your plans. Stairs to the ground should be supported at the bottom by a concrete landing, or at least by concrete footings for the stringers. To determine the landing's height and location, consider it as another stair tread in your overall calculation of stair dimensions. The landing should extend at least 3 feet in front of the bottom step. You can form and pour a landing at the same time as the deck footings, or wait until the deck is completed to be sure the height and location of the landing are accurate.

Calculating the Dimensions

A flight of stairs is made up of risers, treads, and support stringers. Your local building code will stipulate the minimum width (as viewed from the side; also called tread depth) of the stair treads and the maximum height of the risers—typically 10 inches for treads and 7½ inches for risers. The tread width plus twice the riser height should equal between 25 and 26 inches. Note that the tread width dimension refers to the dimension on the stringer; the actual tread width is greater, due to the overhang, usually 1 to 1½ inches. Also, the stairs' total rise divided by the rise of each step must equal a whole number, since all steps must be equal in rise. The width of the stairs should be no less than 36 inches, wide enough for two people to easily pass each other. Note: All of these dimensions are minimum requirements; lower the riser height and widen the treads for safer and more graceful stairways. Just be sure that all of the stairways around a deck have identical riser and tread dimensions.

To determine the number of steps you'll need, measure the vertical distance (the total rise) from the surface of the decking to the ground where the stairs will land. Then divide this distance by the desired riser height, as set by your local building code. For example, if the deck is 48 inches above grade and you plan on using 6-inch risers, you'll need 8 steps exactly. If, however, the deck height divided by the riser height is a whole number plus a fraction, divide that whole number back into the deck height. This will give you the exact riser height you'll need for each step. For example, if the deck is 51 inches high and the riser height you want is 7 inches, the number of steps would be 7.29. The next whole number is 8, so divide that into 51 inches and the new riser height would be 6¾ inches.

To find the exact width of each tread, subtract twice the riser height from 26 inches. For a 6-inch riser, the proper width of the tread is 14 inches—that is, 26 minus 12. Your riser-to-tread ratio is a 6-inch riser to a 14-inch tread. You may want to adjust dimensions so the tread width will

Laying Out a Stringer

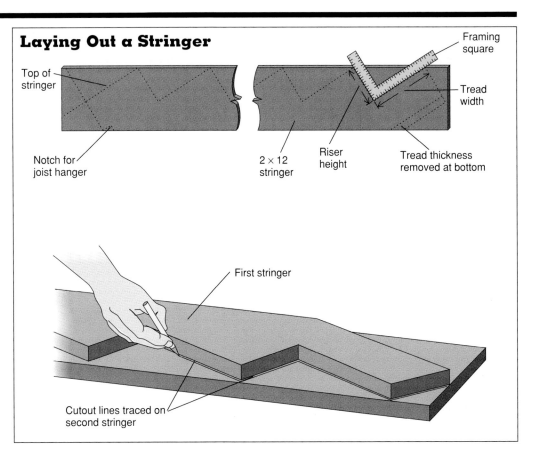

Top of stringer

Notch for joist hanger

2 × 12 stringer

Riser height

Framing square

Tread width

Tread thickness removed at bottom

First stringer

Cutout lines traced on second stringer

be just right for standard lumber dimensions; for example, two 2 by 6s will make an 11¼-inch-wide tread, or two 2 by 6s and a 2 by 4 will make a 14-inch-wide tread.

Finally, you'll need to figure the total run to find out if your measurements will fit the available space. Multiply the tread width by the number of treads. Eight steps with seven 14-inch-wide treads, for example, would have a run of 98 inches.

If the steps don't fit in the space, adjust the riser-to-tread ratio, increasing the riser and decreasing the tread. For safety, all steps must have the same riser-to-tread ratio, and all risers must be within ³⁄₁₆ inch of the same height.

Laying Out the Stringers

Stairs are supported by stringers made from 2 by 12s that are long enough to reach from the top to the bottom level at the proper angle. This size lumber has enough depth for the step notches to be cut out and still carry the load.

Stringers are either cutout or straight styles. Cutout stringers are solid boards with triangular sections removed to accommodate treads and risers. Straight stringers require cleats, brackets, or dadoes to support the treads.

To lay out either type of stringer, you'll first need to determine their length. Measure the total rise (from the top of the footing or cleat to the top of the decking) and

total run of the stairs and mark these distances on a framing square, with the run number on the body of the square and the rise number on its tongue. Measure the distance between these two points to get the length of the stringers, in feet. Add an extra 2 feet to allow for connecting the stringers to the deck and for cutting off a portion for leveling.

Lay out the lines for the cutouts or the location of the tread support on the 2 by 12s using the framing square, with the riser dimension on the tongue and the tread dimension on the body. Line up the marks with the top edge of the 2 by 12 and trace the outline of the risers and treads onto it. Use a knife blade or sharp pencil for tracing, to avoid incremental increases in the riser heights.

Cutting the Stringers

For a cutout stringer, use a circular saw to begin the cuts and, to avoid overcutting, finish the cuts with a handsaw. Because the tread thickness will increase the height of the first step, measure the thickness of a tread and cut away this amount from the bottom of the stringer. This is called dropping the stringer.

Once one stringer is cut, use it as a pattern to cut the other. Then apply preservative to all cut edges.

If you plan to use a straight, or solid, stringer, measure and mark it in the same manner as the cutout stringer. But, instead of cutting away the triangles, use them as guides to attach the cleats or brackets, or to cut the dadoes.

Stringer-to-Deck Connection

To install the stringers, first set them in place for a test fit. Make sure they are parallel and level with each other by measuring the distance between them and by laying a level on them. Then fasten the top of each stringer to the deck substructure with bolts, lag screws, or metal connectors, depending on how the joists are aligned. Attach the bottom of the stringers to the concrete landing or to individual footings. Attach them directly to the concrete with anchor bolts, angle iron, or metal connectors, or attach cleats to the

Designs for Single Steps

Many times a full set of stairs is not required, but only one or two steps. Although these are much easier to build than a full set, you must still observe the basic riser and tread ratio (see page 70). The designs illustrated here are some ways of creating a one-step change of level on a deck, or of creating a one-step access to a deck.

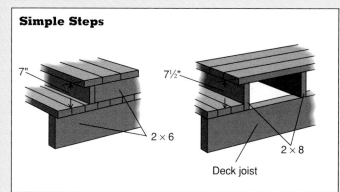

Simple Steps

7"

7½"

2 × 6

2 × 8

Deck joist

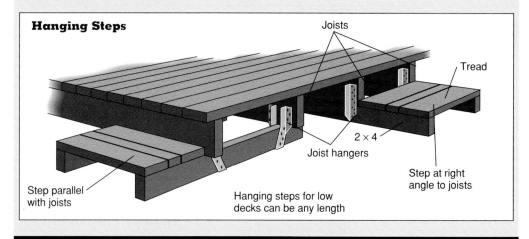

Hanging Steps

Joists

Tread

Step parallel with joists

2 × 4

Joist hangers

Step at right angle to joists

Hanging steps for low decks can be any length

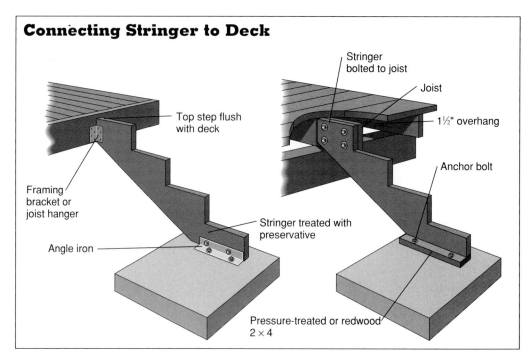

Connecting Stringer to Deck

Stringer bolted to joist

Joist

Top step flush with deck

1½" overhang

Framing bracket or joist hanger

Angle iron

Stringer treated with preservative

Anchor bolt

Pressure-treated or redwood 2 × 4

Attaching Treads

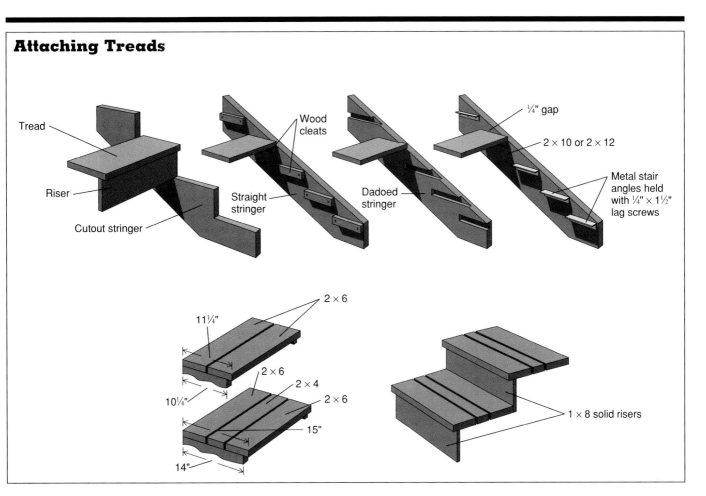

Tread

Riser

Cutout stringer

Wood cleats

Straight stringer

Dadoed stringer

¼" gap

2 × 10 or 2 × 12

Metal stair angles held with ¼" × 1½" lag screws

2 × 6

11¼"

2 × 6

2 × 6

2 × 4

2 × 6

10¼"

15"

14"

1 × 8 solid risers

concrete and toenail the stringers to them with galvanized 12d nails, predrilling first. Any wood that touches the concrete must be pressure-treated lumber or the heartwood of a durable species.

Attaching the Treads

Generally, the riser space is left open to allow air to circulate. However, it can be closed to hide the substructure of the deck by nailing a 1-by riser board across each riser space before installing the tread. Cut the riser boards slightly narrower than the riser height to allow an air space where the bottom corners join the stringer cutouts.

When you cut the tread material to length, the ends of the treads can be flush with the side of the stringer, or they can have a slight overhang. Instead of using one wide board for each step, install two or three narrow boards. The spaces between the boards allow water to drain through, and narrow boards will cup or warp less than a single, wide tread board.

If you are using a cutout stringer, attach the treads directly to the stringer, using 12d galvanized common nails, 16d galvanized spiral-shank nails, or 3-inch deck screws.

If you are using a straight stringer, install and support the treads with cleats, metal brackets, or cutaway dadoes. Attach cleats to the stringers with four 3-inch deck screws in each cleat (use washers to keep the screws from penetrating all the way through the stringer). Attach metal brackets, or stair angles, to the stringer with ¼-inch by 1½-inch galvanized lag screws. Then attach the treads to the cleats or stair angles by driving lag screws up through the cleats or stair angles into the treads.

After installing the treads, round the front edges slightly with a rasping plane, smoothing plane, or sander.

Step 12: Build the Railings

Any deck can benefit from railings. The boundaries and visual lines the railings create add a sense of enclosure, safety, and privacy. Railings can be as formal or as rustic as you like, to match the architectural style of your home. There are numerous railing materials available, but the most common are pressure-treated lumber and redwood.

Before you start, check your local building code. Most codes require that decks 30 inches or higher have railings 36 to 42 inches high, and that all stairs with more than four risers have a railing on each

Railing Configurations

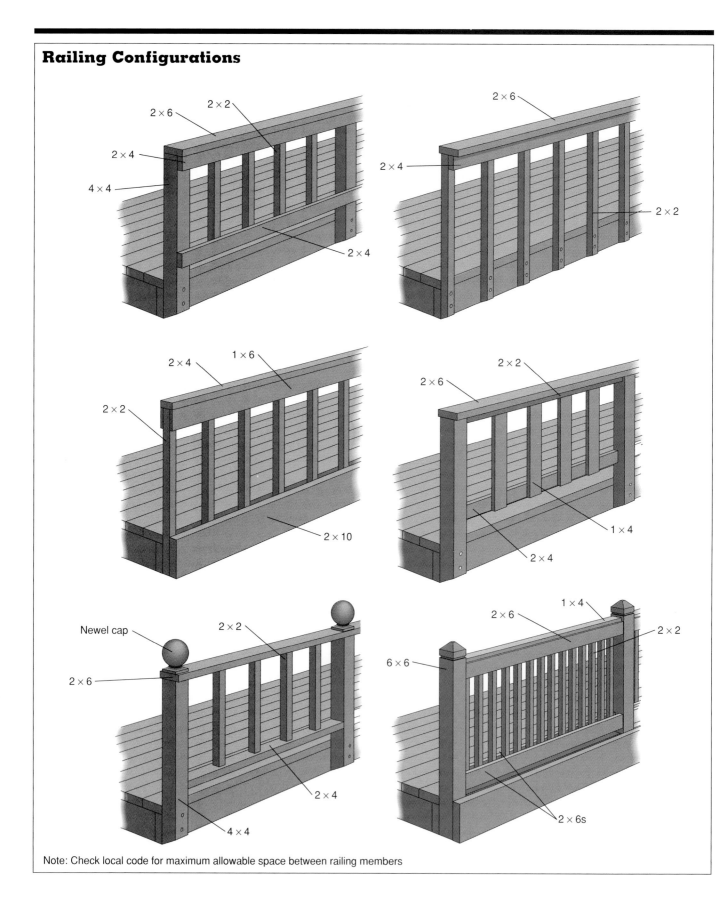

Note: Check local code for maximum allowable space between railing members

74

Railing Configurations

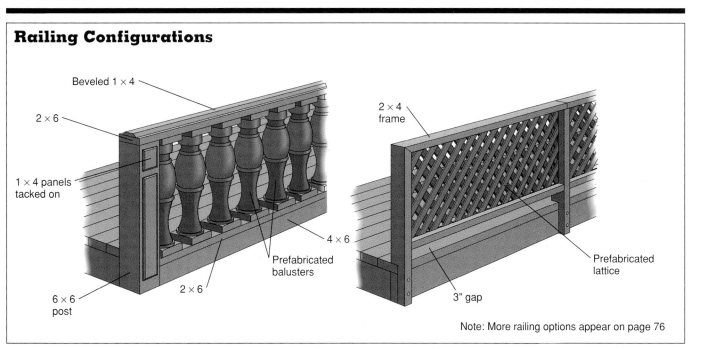

Beveled 1 × 4

2 × 6

1 × 4 panels tacked on

6 × 6 post

2 × 6

Prefabricated balusters

4 × 6

2 × 4 frame

3" gap

Prefabricated lattice

Note: More railing options appear on page 76

open side, 30 to 33 inches above the tread nosings. Spacing between the balusters is closely regulated at 4 to 6 inches, maximum.

Railing Options

Most styles are variations of two simple designs: top and bottom rails with several intermediate rails in between, or top and bottom rails separated by vertical balusters. The top rail can stand on its own, or if you choose, it can be covered with a cap that is mitered at the corners and beveled on top to shed water.

There are several ways to embellish railings. You can add a cap to the top rail, top off the posts with plain or decorative finials, use rounded spindles instead of flat balusters, and fill the space between the rails with screen, cable, lattice, solid wood, canvas, or hard plastic.

Assembling the Railing Components

Assembly techniques vary with the design, but for most railings the process is to cut the posts, rails, balusters, and decorative components to size, then install them as individual pieces, in that order, or fabricate modules that can be installed as a unit.

Posts

The best way to secure railing posts to the deck is to fasten their bottom ends to the outside of the joists, joist header, or beams with carriage bolts or metal connectors.

With a combination square, mark the location of each post according to your deck plans. Then cut each post to length. You may also want to use a circular saw or router to cut embellished tops, such as a peaked chamfer, flat-topped chamfer, routed top, capped top, or an angled top. At the

bottom ends of each post, drill two pilot holes, one above the other. Then slip in the carriage bolts and secure the posts to the header joists and beams. If you want the posts set in from the deck edge, cut out a notch at the bottom. The remaining part of the post should be at least 2 inches thick, and the notch should be no longer than the height of the joist header or fascia board around the edge of the deck. Attach this post the same way as an unnotched post, but with shorter bolts.

You can also attach the posts with half post bases. These metal connectors attach to the decking boards above the joist. You then secure the post in the base with nails or screws.

If your railing posts are simply extensions of the foundation posts, no additional posts may be necessary, but you should check your local building code. Intermediate posts may be required to make

the railing strong enough to sustain a prescribed lateral force, typically 15 pounds per square foot.

Rails and Balusters

Once the posts are installed, add the top, bottom, and any intermediate rails to the inside or outside of the posts.

To install rails between posts, cut them for a snug fit. There are two methods for toenailing them to each post: angling the nails through the rail into the post, or driving the nails through the side of the post into the rail end. Choose whichever method will make the nail heads less obtrusive. For either method, predrill holes through the starting member (rail or post). Use 8d galvanized common nails for nailing the rail to the post, and 12d galvanized common nails for driving through the post into the rail end. With a nail set, countersink each nail head slightly.

Railing Configurations

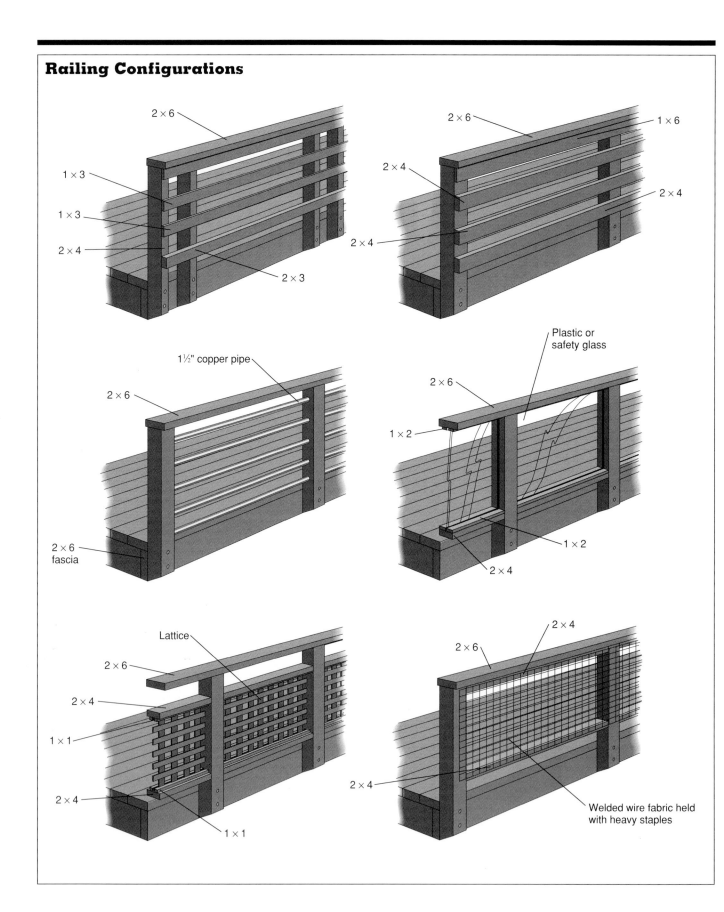

2 × 6

1 × 3

1 × 3

2 × 4

2 × 3

2 × 6

1 × 6

2 × 4

2 × 4

2 × 4

1½" copper pipe

2 × 6

2 × 6
fascia

Plastic or
safety glass

2 × 6

1 × 2

1 × 2

2 × 4

Lattice

2 × 6

2 × 4

1 × 1

2 × 4

1 × 1

2 × 4

2 × 6

2 × 4

Welded wire fabric held
with heavy staples

For cap rails, use the longest lengths of lumber possible. Make sure that any necessary joints will occur over a post; cut joints at a bevel so they overlay slightly. For miter joints at the corners, cut the first piece at a 45-degree angle and nail it in place with two 16d hot-dipped galvanized (HDG) spiral-shank nails facenailed into each post (predrill the cap rail at the ends); lay the second piece in its exact position, with the free end extending over the top of the first piece. Mark a cutting line on the bottom of the second piece by scribing along the 45-degree cut of the first piece. Cut it and nail it in place with 16d HDG spiral-shank nails, predrilling for the nails at the joint. In addition to nails driven into the post, lock-nail the two boards together with an 8d galvanized common nail (predrill).

Here are three easy ways to install balusters. First, you can attach them to the inside, outside, or both sides of the top and bottom rails and facenail them with HDG box nails. Second, you can toenail the top of the balusters up into the top rail and facenail the bottom directly against the joists, joist header, or beams. In this case, no bottom rail is needed. Finally, you can place the ends of the balusters in grooves you cut lengthwise in the rails, then toenail them with 6d galvanized finishing nails. Regardless of how you install the balusters, be sure to space them evenly by using a spacer block cut from a scrap piece of lumber.

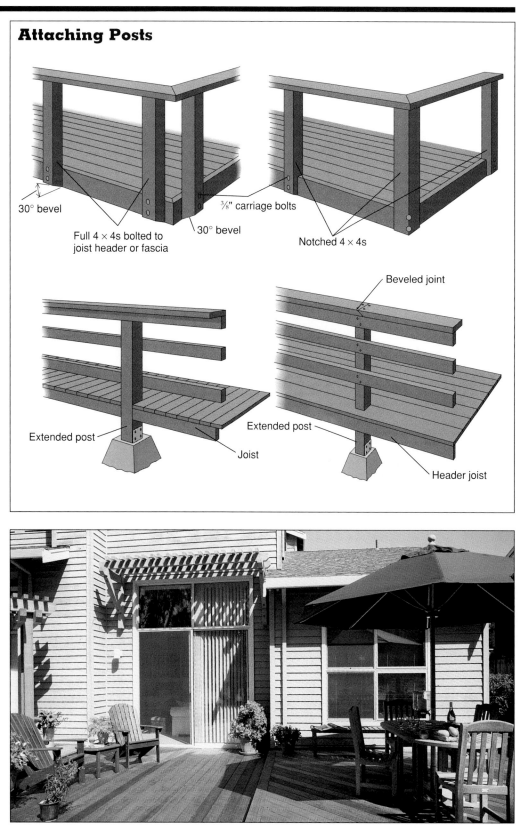

Attaching Posts

30° bevel

Full 4 × 4s bolted to joist header or fascia

30° bevel

⅜" carriage bolts

Notched 4 × 4s

Beveled joint

Extended post

Joist

Extended post

Header joist

This town-house deck, shown under construction on the following two pages, features two levels.

This page: The basic sequence of building a deck has been varied to allow for this site's conditions and the low profile of the deck.

Top: The old doorstep is removed and, after the slope is checked for proper drainage, footing holes are dug. Center left: A grid of ½-inch rebar, held off the ground by 3-inch concrete blocks, is placed in the bottom of each hole. Center right: Concrete, delivered by a pump truck, is placed in each hole, and brackets or piers are set into the wet concrete. Bottom left: Posts are installed, and beams are placed and squared. Bottom right: Where they are close to the ground, the beams are secured directly to the brackets or piers and are leveled with shims or short posts as necessary.

Opposite page: Top left: A ledger is attached to the house for each deck level. Top right: Joists, headers, and blocking are installed over the beams. Center left: Strips of building paper protect the tops of beams and joists. Center right: Decking is attached with deck clips. Bottom left: Stairs are built, and a border is added around the edge of the decking. Bottom right: The railing is installed.

The finished deck is shown on page 77.

AFTER YOUR DECK IS BUILT

Now that the deck is constructed, you may be anxious to pull out the grill and hold your first party. But before you expose the deck to the wearing effects of foot traffic and family use, it needs one final touch—the finish.

Finishing is the first and most important step you will take toward maintaining the deck. A deck must endure water, mildew, fungi, bacteria, ultraviolet rays, fluctuating temperatures, and foot traffic. The proper finish can shield the deck from all these elements. There is a variety of products to choose from; the one you select dictates just how easy or difficult maintaining the deck will be later.

This chapter also includes tips and guidelines for keeping new decks in good condition and for making older decks more attractive, including regular maintenance, repairs, restoration, and an occasional refinishing.

As you use your deck, you may find that some added touches would make it more functional and enjoyable. The chapter ends with ideas for enhancing the deck.

This deck could have been a simple outdoor platform, but with the addition of benches, planters, screens, lights, a food-preparation center, and a spa, it is now a complete outdoor entertainment "room."

THE FINISHING TOUCH

Your choice of a deck finish is a matter of aesthetic preference and maintenance requirements. The proper finish, coupled with regular maintenance, will keep the deck looking its best for years.

Weathered or Not

If you want the deck to have a gray, weathered look, don't do anything—the sun's ultraviolet rays will produce this effect naturally. The best woods for natural weathering are pressure-treated lumber and better grades of cedar, cypress, and redwood.

Generally, it takes two years to complete the weathering process. However, you can age the wood to the gray you want, perhaps in only several months, then slow the aging by treating the wood with a water sealer. This is a good idea even for pressure-treated lumber, since continuous exposure to the elements without a coat of protection leads to premature rotting, swelling, and splitting. To accelerate the weathering process, use a wood bleach or a specialty product for weathering decks, following the manufacturer's instructions.

The final color depends on the species of lumber. Cedar and cypress weather to a light silvery gray; redwood turns dark gray; pressure-treated lumber turns a lighter shade of its original color.

Using Finishes

Wood is so vulnerable to weather, ultraviolet light, insects, mold, mildew, and foot traffic that there's no surefire way to protect it permanently from all these factors. You can, however, slow the process considerably with a protective finish.

There are several types to choose from: wood preservatives, sealers, semitransparent stains, solid stains, and paints. Which one is right for your deck depends on the species and grade of lumber it is made of, how the deck will be used, the typical weather conditions in your area, and whether or not you want to change the wood's color, or add color, for effect.

Choosing the proper finishing product should not be a guessing game, yet there are so many different finishes on the market today, you may be overwhelmed by the options and combinations. Some combine wood preservatives with water sealers; others couple sealers with stains. Some products even contain ultraviolet light absorbers and inhibitors, fungicides, mildewcides, and insecticides.

But the variety gives you plenty of design options. You could choose a finish that lets the wood weather naturally to an appealing gray, or one that preserves the wood's natural color. You could even combine finishes for a unique visual effect, painting the substructure and staining the decking, for instance.

Finishes that become slippery when wet are not appropriate around spas and pools. And wood finished with only a water sealer can't withstand a hot, blanching southern sun. "Choosing a Finish," on page 85, is a handy chart that outlines the advantages and disadvantages of each type of finish. Once you've pinpointed which type you would like to use, visit your local home-improvement store. Learn as much as you can about the various products available. Read the product labels and manufacturers' pamphlets. If you use more than one product, make sure all are chemically compatible. Products from the same manufacturer are most likely formulated to work together, but always check the labels for exceptions.

Before any finish can be applied, the wood must be completely dried, or cured. Check with this simple test: Sprinkle water onto a board. If the water is quickly absorbed, the

How Weather Exposure Affects Wood

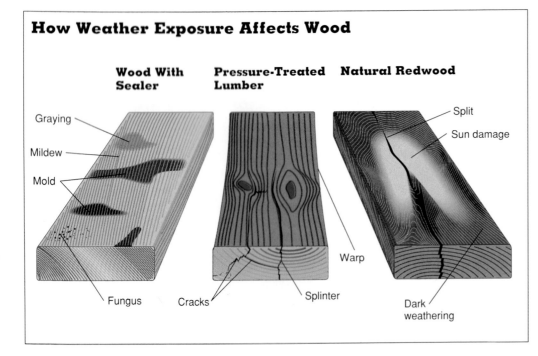

Wood With Sealer
- Graying
- Mildew
- Mold
- Fungus

Pressure-Treated Lumber
- Cracks
- Splinter

Natural Redwood
- Split
- Sun damage
- Warp
- Dark weathering

Finishing Tips

•To save time, money, and frustration, read product labels before you buy. Compare their information about use, coverage, chemical compatibility with other finishes, surface preparation, recommended temperatures and weather conditions for application, application techniques, drying times, recommended number of coats, cleanup, storage, disposal of leftovers, and maintenance.

•Make sure the surface to be finished is clean, dry, and free of dust, loose paint, mold, and mildew. Other-wise, the finish will not adhere properly. Dirt and loose paint will make the surface rough and unattractive. Remove mold and mildew with a fungicide or mildewcide especially made for this purpose.

•If possible, don't apply the finish in direct sunlight, on a windy day, or if rain is forecast. For the finish to adhere properly, it must dry slowly; hot sun dries the finish too quickly. A windless, dry day is ideal because there is less chance of dust and rainwater damaging the finish.

•Always follow manufacturer's instructions. Use a brush, roller, paint pad, or airless sprayer to apply finishes. Wood pieces can also be dipped prior to assembly.

•Protect yourself and the environment. Wear rubber gloves and safety goggles. Be sure to read, understand, and follow the cautions, first-aid instructions, and other safety information printed on labels. Dispose of leftover products and rags according to the label and your local environmental ordinances.

wood is ready for finishing. If the water is not absorbed, give it more time to cure.

Wood Preservatives

Wood preservatives protect the deck from insects, rot, mildew, and mold, but they don't protect against moisture or preserve the wood's color. Pressure-treated lumber already contains preservatives, and its factory treatment outmatches do-it-yourself applications. But if you use cedar or cypress and you plan to stain or paint it, you will want to consider using a wood preservative. Some water sealers

Application Techniques

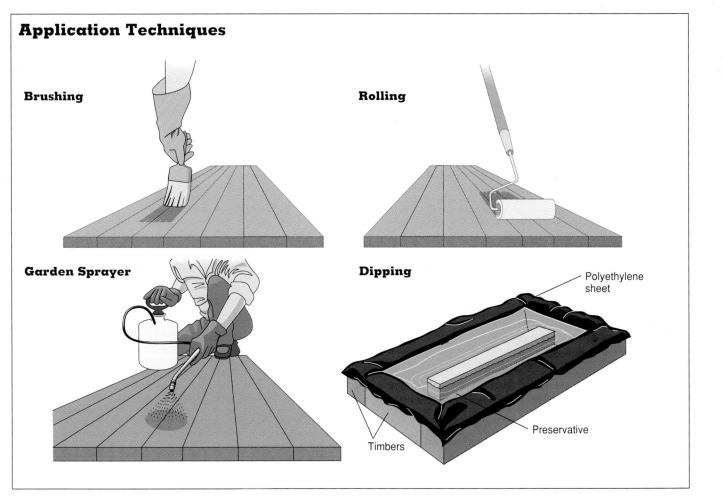

Brushing

Rolling

Garden Sprayer

Dipping

Polyethylene sheet

Preservative

Timbers

and stains contain a wood preservative.

Use products that are both effective and safe. Pentachlorophenol, creosote, and arsenic compounds have been banned for health and environmental reasons. One relatively safe, effective, and environmentally acceptable wood preservative is copper naphthenate. It's nontoxic to plants and animals, so it is particularly useful in finishing planters and garden structures. It is available in a clear form, or in a green color that leaves the wood with a green tinge, which will fade as the wood weathers. Renewing the treatment every couple of years maintains the protection.

Apply wood preservatives with a brush, or a roller with a 1-inch nap. Always read the manufacturer's instructions and wear rubber gloves and safety glasses. If you are constructing a small item, such as a planter, you can immerse the boards in a trough of preservative before assembling them.

Sealers

Sealers, or water repellents, are waterlike finishes that serve two purposes. They penetrate the wood to prevent it from absorbing water, which would cause swelling, cracking, and warping. They also help retain wood's natural look and color longer by temporarily delaying the weathering process that inevitably turns it gray.

Sealers can be applied to all species of wood and pressure-treated lumber. Some products seal and stain in one step. Sealers with ultraviolet light absorbers provide extra protection against the sun's bleaching effect. Avoid sealers that form hard surfaces, which can become slippery. In addition to the safety concerns they raise, their surfaces will eventually crack as the wood expands and contracts, leaving the deck vulnerable to water damage.

Stains

Unlike paints, stains penetrate deep into the wood. Rather than concealing the grain pattern, they enhance it. Some stains contain preservatives and sealers, protecting the wood from water, mildew, insects, and the effects of ultraviolet light.

There are two kinds of stains available: semitransparent (or light bodied) and solid (or full bodied). Semitransparent stains contain less pigment than solid stains, so the beauty of the wood shows through naturally, and prematurely weathered or worn areas that develop are hard to notice. Use semitransparent stains on the decking boards if they have few or no flaws.

If the decking material is of low-grade lumber with lots of flaws, solid stains make an

A clear preservative, renewed every few years, enhances the deep color and rich grain pattern of this redwood decking.

A light-bodied stain applied to this deck ensures uniform pigmentation and, by matching the color of the house, ties the deck to it.

Choosing a Finish

Type of Finish	Advantages	Disadvantages
Wood Preservative Principal ingredient is copper naphthenate, an environmentally approved chemical that turns the wood a deep greenish color, which eventually fades.	Soaks into wood. Resists decay and insects. Wood can be stained, painted, sealed, or allowed to weather naturally.	Not water resistant. Wood should also be coated with sealer for moisture protection. Do-it-yourself treatment not as thorough and durable as factory pressure treatment.
Sealer Also called a water repellent. Available in oil-based and water-based types. Oil-based sealers are more durable and suitable for decks. May be applied to all wood species and to pressure-treated lumber. For maximum protection, apply 2 thin coats. May be added to oil-based paints or stains; check compatibility. Do not add to water-based paint or stain.	Penetrates into wood to form protective barrier. Helps minimize formation of water stains. Reduces warping, splitting, shrinking, and swelling of the wood. Delays natural weathering process that turns wood gray. Some sealers are specifically formulated to retain natural color and texture of a particular species. Surface coating is durable, not easily abraded. Dries clear, unless pigment added. Some contain fungicides and mildewcides. Some contain ultraviolet light inhibitors, absorbers, or blockers. Both oil-based and water-based stains and paints may be applied over sealers.	Not effective on previously stained or painted surfaces because it is unable to penetrate the wood properly. Toxic to fish and wildlife. You must take care not to contaminate water when cleaning equipment, and dispose of container and rags properly.
Stain Semitransparent and solid stains protect and add color. There are oil-based and water-based types. Some are specially formulated for use on decks. Choose a nonchalking type and possibly one with a sealer or preservative added.	Penetrates into wood to protect it from damaging moisture and the bleaching effects of ultraviolet light. Adds color. Comes in many assorted colors or may be custom mixed to match or complement your home. Easy to apply.	The color is sometimes unpredictable because it's influenced by the species, grade, color, and condition of the wood. Always test the color in an inconspicuous place or on a piece of leftover lumber. Must be renewed, usually once a year.
Semitransparent Stain Also called light-bodied stain. Contains a small amount of pigment. Resulting color is blend of 2 colors—the stain and the wood.	Lets the wood grain and texture show through for a more natural look. Best choice for the surface of the decking and stairs. Weathered and worn areas will be less noticeable as the deck ages. Suitable for new or previously stained wood in the same semitransparent color range.	Can't be applied to wood that is painted or stained with a solid stain. Overlap marks will occur if you fail to work from a wet to a dry area. Ideally, stain the full length of each board at a time. Requires periodic reapplication to keep the benefits of the stain effective.
Solid Stain Also called full-bodied stain. Contains heavy pigment that acts and looks like paint. Reapply as needed to keep deck looking attractive.	Contains more pigment than semitransparent stains. Hides flaws, knots, grain patterns, and the wood's condition. Ideal for low grades of lumber. Lets the texture of the wood show through. Quite durable. Suitable for new, old, stained, or weathered wood.	Shows premature wear in high-traffic areas such as stairs and deck surface.
Paint Available in oil-based and water-based types. Choose a nonchalking type and one that is specially formulated for decks so it withstands the abuse of foot traffic. Reapply when worn, faded, peeling, or chipped.	Ideal for refinishing older decks or low grades of lumber. Hides flaws, knots, grain, and the condition of the wood. Integrates deck constructed from several different woods. Durable, stain resistant, and moisture resistant. Marine grades are most durable and expensive. Unlimited colors. Coordinates deck with house.	Generally more time consuming to apply. More expensive than other types of finishes. Once painted, components can only be repainted. Slippery when wet—mix in silica sand for traction. Tends to crack as wood contracts and expands repeatedly.

excellent finish. Since they have some of the characteristics of paint, they hide the wood grain and imperfections, and they are quite durable. When choosing a stain, select a nonchalking or sealer type made for decks. Stains that contain chalk leave an unsightly powdery film on the wood's surface.

To ensure consistent color, check that the batch numbers on all of the cans are alike; if custom-mixing, have all the cans mixed at the same time. If you are staining pressure-treated wood, select a stain formulated especially for this purpose.

How the stain will color the deck cannot be predicted by a store's sample or color chip. The wood's species, grade, condition, and natural color will affect the stain, so before you do the entire deck, test the color on an inconspicuous place.

Allow pressure-treated lumber and woods that have already been treated with preservative or sealer to weather for at least 90 days prior to complete application.

Two thin coats are more durable than a single thick one. For smooth, consistent color, apply the stain evenly without overlaps, and wipe off any excess.

Paints

Paint hides knots and other imperfections better than any other type of finish, making it ideal for use on low-grade lumber. However, paint takes longer to apply than other finishes, and is more expensive and harder to maintain. If you plan to use low-grade lumber

for the decking surface, then cover its flaws with paint, the money you save in lumber will probably be spent on the finish. Once you've painted the deck, you are committed to a paint finish in the future, because after the wood's pores have been filled with paint pigments, it is impossible to return them to a natural wood finish.

Paradoxically, paint's good coverage makes it a poor choice of finish for the decking

surface. It inevitably wears away under foot traffic, creating noticeable patterns across the deck, and its smooth surface tends to crack when the wood expands and contracts. It may be wisest to reserve paint for the deck's structural underpinnings.

If you do choose to paint the deck surface, find a product formulated for the wear and tear a deck endures; a self-priming alkyd-based deck

paint is a good choice. Regular exterior acrylic paints just cannot hold up, and they peel and chip easily.

A painted deck surface is quite slippery when wet. You can remedy this by mixing silica sand into the paint before applying the final coat to high-traffic areas, such as the stairs and entrances. Read the directions on the bag for mixing instructions and coverage.

Paint doesn't have to be bright and bold—neutral colors give this deck a fresh appeal.

MAINTENANCE, REPAIR, AND RESTORATION

Wood damage caused by weather changes, moisture, ultraviolet light, insects, decay, and normal wear all contribute to the gradual deterioration of your deck. You can delay this eventuality with routine cleaning and maintenance.

Routine Maintenance

To keep repairs manageable, and the deck sound and attractive, establish a regular maintenance schedule. Get in the habit of sweeping, hosing off, and scrubbing the deck's surface on a weekly or monthly basis. For a more thorough cleaning, perhaps once a season, rent a pressure washer to remove dirt, loose paint, and debris that accumulates in the gaps between the decking boards and the joints of the deck's components. The cleaning not only removes harmful dirt and grime, it gives the deck a fresh, new look. Rent a washer that generates around 1,200 pounds per square inch (psi)—higher pressures aren't necessary for decks. The jet of water from a pressure washer is potentially dangerous. Follow instructions from the manufacturer and rental agent carefully. Do not point the wand at unprotected skin, and wear rubber gloves and eye protection.

Every few years, or as often as necessary, renew the finish to keep the deck attractive and to ensure protection against the elements. Check the finish label for the recommended reapplication times and mark them on a calendar.

Inspect deck components, stairs, railings, and built-in accessories regularly for evidence of damage or deterioration. Watch for mold and mildew, as well as termites and other pests. Locate the cause of these problems—perhaps as simple as puddles forming under the planters—and fix it immediately. A small problem caught in time can prevent a large one or an unsafe condition from developing later.

Carefully inspect railings, tables, benches, and other accessories that come in contact with clothing and skin. Keep them clean and free of splinters, and watch for signs of deterioration that could make them unsafe when people lean or sit on them.

Maintaining Stairs

Deck stairs that lead to the yard are one of the first places to show signs of wear. Under the duress of heavy foot traffic, dirt and debris wear down the finish and eventually grind away exposed wood fibers.

Sweep and hose off the stairs often to keep most of the dirt and debris from becoming a problem. It's also important to renew the finish often, perhaps every season, depending on how much foot traffic the stairs must endure.

To slow down tread wear, install self-adhesive, nonskid strips on each step. They also make the steps safer, especially when wet, and they are inexpensive and easy to find at home-improvement centers.

Maintaining the Decking

Dirt and debris build up between the decking boards, locking in moisture and preventing air from circulating. Eventually, this causes mold and mildew to develop and leads to premature wood rot and decay. Regularly sweep and hose down the deck to prevent dirt and debris from building up, then dislodge stubborn debris between boards with a putty knife or wire brush.

Exposure to ultraviolet light, traffic patterns, shade from trees and roof overhangs, and the placement of accessories all contribute to uneven weathering and wear of the deck's surface. Revive the wood by scrubbing it with oxalic acid, or a product that contains this chemical; follow the manufacturer's instructions carefully. After cleaning, apply a fresh coat of finish, preferably one that contains an ultraviolet light blocker, absorber, or inhibitor.

To prevent further uneven weathering and traffic paths from forming, occasionally rearrange planters, benches, tables, chairs, and other portable items.

Excess water runoff, standing water, splashing from a spa, and dampness create unsightly water stains, especially on the surface of the decking. Scrub stains with oxalic acid, or a product containing this chemical, then apply a waterproofing sealer to protect against future stains. Follow the manufacturer's instructions for both products. To avoid recurrence of the problem, try to eliminate the cause of the moisture. If that's not possible, reapply the sealer every six months or as needed for ongoing protection.

When caught early, stains from dirt, leaves, and other debris can usually be scrubbed away with trisodium phosphate (TSP). Be sure to follow the manufacturer's instructions carefully.

Keeping the Weathered Look

If you want your deck to have a weathered look, you need only apply a sealer. The ultraviolet rays from the sun turn the wood from its natural color to a weathered gray. The sealer repels moisture but won't interfere with the natural weathering process—as long as you use a brand that doesn't contain ultraviolet light blockers, inhibitors, or absorbers, which are specifically used to prevent weathering.

If you want to accelerate the weathering process and achieve a more uniform look, apply a wood bleach, using a brand that contains a mildewcide. (If the deck surface has had a recent application of preservative or sealer, or is made of pressure-treated lumber, wait at least 60 days before applying bleach.) Brush or roll on the bleach, then wait the specified period of time before hosing it off, according to the manufacturer's instructions. Renew the bleach treatment periodically as the deck darkens.

Restoring the Natural Look

When a deck is first built, it has a warm, natural color. Over time, the ultraviolet light from the sun changes it to a weathered gray. It's possible to restore a deck to its natural tone, assuming it has been left unsealed.

First, scrub it with TSP to remove dirt, debris, and fungi. Then apply oxalic acid or a special deck-renewing product formulated for this purpose. Follow manufacturers' instructions carefully. The deck will quickly change from weathered gray to its natural color, although, because of aging and wearing, the wood will not have a crisp, new look. To help retain the natural color, apply a sealer that blocks out ultraviolet light. When the deck begins to turn gray again, repeat the process.

Mold and Mildew Remedies

Wood discolors from mold and mildew and becomes slippery when wet. Mold and mildew are also unsightly and can eventually lead to wood decay. Lack of ventilation and excess moisture from standing water are the main causes of mold and mildew. Ineffective finishes and lack of maintenance also contribute to the problem. Fortunately, the solutions are relatively simple.

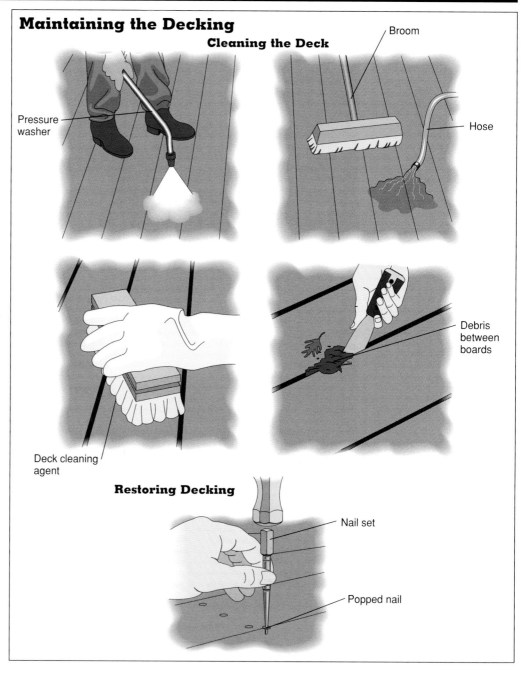

Maintaining the Decking

Cleaning the Deck

Broom

Pressure washer

Hose

Deck cleaning agent

Debris between boards

Restoring Decking

Nail set

Popped nail

Standing water—puddles collecting in indentations and cupping on the surface of the decking—can be the result of poorly directed runoff water and melting snow. You should be able to improve the situation by channeling water runoff with a gutter and downspout system.

Good ventilation requires air circulation between the decking and the substructure, which can be inhibited by debris caught between the decking boards. Remove the debris with a stiff brush or pressure washer.

Once the deck components become damp or wet, humid weather may prevent them from drying out, resulting in an ideal environment for mold and mildew. These fungi also grow under planters, benches, tables, and chairs, if they stay damp for a long time. Routinely move anything portable, to let the areas underneath dry. To retard the growth of fungi, clean the

Replacing Decking

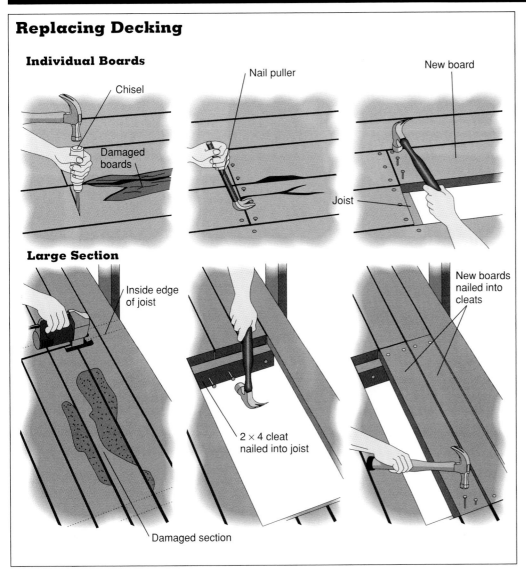

Individual Boards

Chisel

Damaged boards

Nail puller

New board

Joist

Large Section

Inside edge of joist

New boards nailed into cleats

2 × 4 cleat nailed into joist

Damaged section

deck regularly with a mildew-cide or fungicide, avoiding products that contain bleach, which will discolor the wood. TSP is ideal; it's easy to use and readily available. Follow with a finish that contains, again, a mildewcide or fungicide.

Deterring Termites and Other Pests

Probably the most commonly known wood-destroying insects are termites and carpenter ants. They eat wood

fibers, which, of course, undermines the lumber's strength. There are two types of termites that pose particular problems. Dry wood termites, seldom seen until it's too late, bore tunnels in the wood and hollow out large chambers; subterranean termites invade wood from below ground and can be detected only if they leave telltale earth tubes or are present in large numbers.

Pressure-treated lumber contains preservatives that

deter wood-damaging ants, termites, and other insects. To add to its effectiveness, apply a wood preservative to any end grain. If the termite infestation is severe, and treating the wood fails to deter them, consider chemically treating the soil under and around the deck. Check with your local home-improvement center for products that best suit your needs. Read labels carefully and always follow manufacturers' instructions.

Repair and Restoration

When the deck begins to show signs of wear and damage, take time to repair and replace worn components. Otherwise, as they continue to deteriorate, they will become unsightly and unsafe.

Nails

Two main problems are caused by nails: staining and rising up. Obviously, steel nails will cause rust stains, but galvanized nails sometimes leave stains, too. This happens if the protective coating was cracked during installation, or if it wears away.

Remove rust stains with oxalic acid, or a product containing the chemical. Scrub away the stains following the manufacturer's instructions. The effect will be temporary; the stains will return eventually. Make removing rust stains part of your routine maintenance plan.

Nails that have protruding heads should be reset as soon as possible for appearance and safety. Check for raised nails as part of your routine maintenance, too.

Decking

Even with proper maintenance, pieces of decking may crack or wear to the point they need replacing. Usually, problems first appear at the ends of boards and at end-to-end joints, where the end grain is more vulnerable to weather and wear.

Begin by hosing off or pressure washing the decking boards so you can carefully inspect them. If parts of the decking are deteriorated—either an individual board or a large section—you can remove and replace them easily.

To remove an individual board, simply pry it loose from its joists. If only a portion of the board is damaged, cut out the area with a hammer and wood chisel, or remove the entire board and cut away the damaged section. Cut away the deteriorated board only over its joists, where the ends of the replacement board will be positioned and nailed. Every replacement piece you insert must have its ends supported by the joists; otherwise, it will deteriorate rapidly and cup, creating a precarious walking surface. If it's not possible to do this, add supports by securing blocking between the joists.

To remove large sections of decking, first locate the joists that support the area and mark their inside edges on the surface of the decking. Next, at one corner of the damaged area drill a hole large enough to accommodate the blade of a handheld jigsaw or saber saw. Cut out the sections, being careful to avoid joists, nails, hardware, electrical wires, or plumbing connections. Use a hammer and chisel to remove any remaining ends of the pieces.

While the decking is removed and the structural components are exposed, inspect the joists and beams. Correct any damage (see the following section).

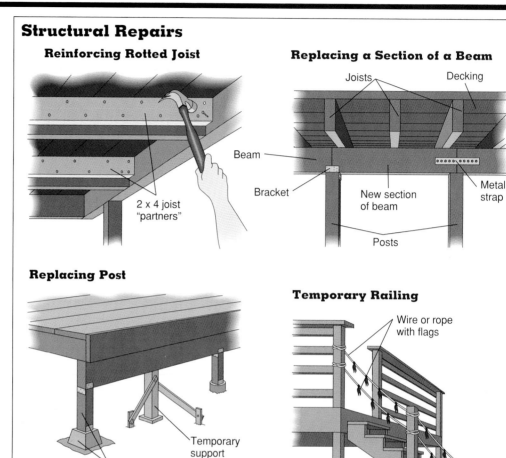

Structural Repairs

Reinforcing Rotted Joist

2 x 4 joist "partners"

Replacing a Section of a Beam

Joists

Decking

Beam

Bracket

New section of beam

Metal strap

Posts

Replacing Post

Replacement post and pier

Temporary support

Temporary Railing

Wire or rope with flags

To complete the repair, cut replacement boards to length and fasten them in place over the joists using galvanized nails. If any of the pieces sit higher than the surrounding pieces, sink the nails and belt-sand the new boards level. Apply finish to the new pieces.

To repair a rough or damaged spot on the surface of the deck, lightly sand the area, being careful not to create indentations that will collect water, and apply the finish. Feather the finish so it blends into the surrounding area.

Joists and Beams

Unusual squeaks and creaks, low spots on the surface of the decking, and cracking are all indications of problems underneath the deck. If you have access to the area, check the joists and beams regularly for damage, rot, decay, and insect infestation, all of which adversely affect the structural integrity of the deck. Any time you remove sections or pieces of the decking, always inspect the exposed joists and beams.

If you find a rotted or decayed joist, remove the decking boards above with a pry bar. A joist with minimal rot can easily be strengthened by a "partner." This is a piece of treated wood attached directly to one side of the rotted joist for added support. Before attaching the partner, treat the source of the joist rot—such as trapped debris that's holding moisture—and make sure there's a solid area in the old joist into which you can nail or screw the partner. The top of the partner must be level with the top of the original joist. Reinstall the decking.

If the damage is severe, the remedy is not easy (another argument for routine maintenance). Left untreated, rotting joists will deteriorate to the point where they must be replaced, and you may also have to replace the decking boards or recut them to new lengths. To replace a joist, install a new one—in the same way you installed the original—parallel to the damaged joist and 4 to 5 inches away from it; the gap prevents the rot from transferring to the new joist. As necessary, replace the decking or cut it to different lengths to accommodate the new joist location.

Beams with a small amount of surface damage can be repaired by the same partner method used to repair joists. Since the beams are major load-bearing components, any that have significant deterioration must be addressed immediately. Depending on the location of the damage, the beam may be replaced entirely or in sections.

To replace only sections, first support the joists above the beams with temporary bracing. Then remove or hacksaw nails that connect the joists to the beam. Cut away the affected area with a saber saw or jigsaw, being careful to avoid cutting into the joists. Make the cuts over the centers of the posts, so the replacement beam will have support. Cut a new piece of beam to length and treat it with preservative and finish, saturating the end grain, which is vulnerable to water damage. Secure the piece over the posts with metal straps and brackets, then remove the temporary bracing and toenail each joist to the new beam with three 8d common nails, or secure them with hurricane ties.

Replacing the entire beam involves supporting all the joists with bracing, dismantling and removing the beam from the posts, and placing and securing a new beam. Your local building inspector should be able to explain exactly how extensive the repair and replacement job should be.

Posts

Replacing a damaged post is not as difficult as it may appear. First, make a temporary post that will support the deck while you make the repair. Nail together two 2 by 4s, and to one end nail a scrap piece of lumber to serve as a base that holds the temporary post steady. Cut the temporary post to length and position it near the damaged post, but leave enough room so you can easily maneuver. Toenail the temporary post in place, adding bracing to stabilize it. Next, remove the damaged post in one piece, if possible; otherwise, saw the post in half and remove it in pieces. Install the new post on the same pier as the original. If the pier does not have a post anchor or bracket, drill a hole into the top with a hammer drill and masonry bit and bolt a post base to the pier. If the old pier is weak or too low, remove it and pour a new footing for a new pier. After installing the new post, remove the temporary post and bracing.

Stairs and Railings

Damaged, rotted, or loose stairs and railings are not only unsightly but, more important, unsafe. When you see evidence that a deck component is deteriorated, replace it immediately.

Replace damaged stair treads or sections of railing by simply making and installing new ones. Replacing damaged stringers requires dismantling the entire run of stairs, building a new set of stringers, and reassembling the components.

A safety reminder: When you are working on stairs or railings, erect a barricade around the entire area to prevent accidents.

A sealer protects wood but allows a natural weathering process.

FILLING THE SPACE

The right additional touches can turn your deck into an outdoor room, so you can, for instance, entertain, relax in privacy, store away yard tools, and enjoy the outdoors after dark. Here are complete instructions for three easy build-it-yourself accessories, plus ideas for others.

Ideas for Overheads, Screens, and Skirts

You can increase the individuality, privacy, and appearance of the deck with overheads, screens, and skirts. Overheads provide shade, screens assure privacy, and skirts hide the substructure of the deck. These additions will give the deck a more tailored look and define the perimeter of your outdoor room.

Overheads

Open or solid overheads serve a variety of purposes. They add to the aesthetics and usefulness of a deck by filtering sunlight, creating shade, and shielding the deck from rain. Climbing roses or vines on an overhead add shade, color, and beauty to the deck area. Cover all or just part of the deck area to create a sense of privacy for entertaining, sunbathing, or a spa. An overhead can be designed to link the yard or house to the deck by creating a covered walkway.

The structural requirements for an open design overhead are not as strict as those for a solid one. Regardless of the design you choose,

check with your local building inspector for requirements.

The most sturdy design is one in which deck posts extend all the way up to support the overhead. The components of an overhead are posts, beams, and rafters, and a ledger board if the overhead is attached to another structure. These components serve the same function as those of a deck but the cross-members are called rafters instead of joists.

To assure the strength and integrity of the overhead, follow the same span tables used to determine the deck's beam and joist spans (see pages 17 and 18). The lowest component of a standard overhead should be the height of a typical doorway, or 80 inches. To provide lateral stability, install a 24-inch 2 by 4 diagonal brace in each corner, where the beam connects to the post. Cut the ends of the braces at a 45-degree angle.

The most common overheads are made entirely of wood, using 4 by 4 posts and 2-by lumber, preferably the same species used for the deck.

Wood used in combination with other materials works well, too. Strips of canvas hung between the rafters or colorful awnings add flare. Ready-made lattice panels attached to the top and sides

of the overhead create an interesting light-filtering effect. Inexpensive bamboo or reed panels can be laid in a pattern across the rafters.

No matter what style and type of overhead you choose, plan ahead, especially if the purpose of the overhead is to create shade. Note where the shade will be cast at different times of the day and year. Also consider wind, heavy snow, rain, and other similar conditions unique to your area that would affect the strength of the overhead you build.

Privacy Screens

As the name implies, privacy screens provide seclusion. They also block sun, wind, rain, and noise. Basic screen construction consists of 4 by 4 posts with various types and sizes of panels attached.

Generally, the panels are made of lattice or of slats arranged in vertical, horizontal, or diagonal patterns. Fence panels available at home-improvement centers make easy-to-install privacy screens.

Deck Skirts

There are two good reasons for adding deck skirts to your finished deck. They enhance the overall appearance of a raised deck by hiding the area underneath, and they keep children and small animals from crawling under the deck.

Skirts are made from lattice or strips of the same wood used for the deck. Be sure to space the strips far enough apart to allow air circulation underneath the deck. Don't use a solid material, such as plywood, which would block the passage of air.

Wood grilles allow air to circulate under this deck, which has skirts made from solid-board siding.

Installing 120V Receptacles

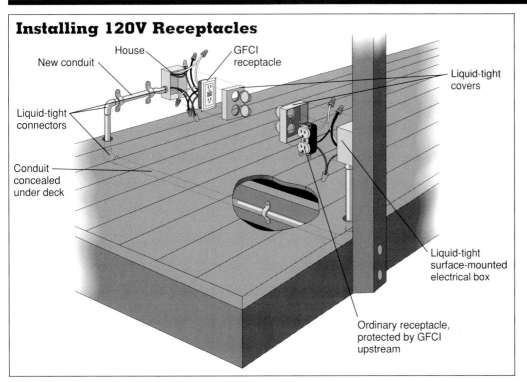

New conduit

House

GFCI receptacle

Liquid-tight connectors

Conduit concealed under deck

Liquid-tight covers

Liquid-tight surface-mounted electrical box

Ordinary receptacle, protected by GFCI upstream

You might build a hinged panel on one side of the deck to allow easy access for maintenance, repairs, weed control, and storage.

Spas

Most of the spas used in decks are the portable type made of durable acrylic. They take relatively little time to install, and since they're portable, they can be packed up and moved when you do.

In most areas, a building permit is not necessary for a portable spa, but the installation itself must comply with the local building and electrical codes.

A portable spa can sit directly on the deck; a built-in spa can be recessed flush with the deck surface. For an on-deck spa, the deck must be structurally able to support the weight of the spa plus the

water. A recessed spa sits on the ground or on a platform below the surface of the deck, and the decking is installed around it.

Consult with a spa professional regarding installation, weight, and the stress that the spa places on a deck or platform. How-to books on installing spas are another valuable source of information.

Lighting and Wiring

Outdoor lighting and electrical outlets increase the deck's versatility. Lighting allows the deck to be used day and night and provides added nighttime security. Outlets for a television, radio, telephone, lights, and other appliances will turn the deck into a genuine outdoor room.

Low-Voltage Lighting

Unlike standard 120-volt lighting that tends to glare and overlight an area, low-voltage lighting is more subtle. It is also decorative, economical, and safe. Another advantage is that you can install it after the deck is completed.

Home-improvement centers sell low-voltage lighting kits that make installation an easy and practical do-it-yourself project. A 12-volt system consists of light fixtures, outdoor cable, and a transformer. Just run the cable, attach the light fixtures, and plug the transformer into an ordinary 120-volt outlet. The transformer reduces the 120-volt current to a softer, safer, and more economical 12 volts.

The cable can be hidden under the outside perimeter of the deck, or elsewhere. The

light fixtures come in specific types for post tops, balusters, rails, benches, planters, landscaped areas, walkways, and anywhere you need soft light.

Electrical Outlets

Whenever electrical devices are used outdoors, the potential for electrical shock exists. To protect against this danger, electrical codes require that the outdoor outlets be protected by a ground fault circuit interrupter (GFCI). The GFCI is designed to trip if the cords on lights, appliances, and tools are in poor repair and could provide a path for current to leak to the ground. The GFCI you install must be rated in amperes and volts to match the rating of the outlet or circuit it is to protect.

The GFCI is insurance against the dangers of electrical shock. It is not a substitute for grounding, however; it is only supplementary protection that senses leakage of currents too small to trigger ordinary fuses or circuit breakers. The GFCI will not prevent a person from receiving a shock, but it will open the circuit so quickly that the shock will be below the level that would inhibit the ability to "let go" of the circuit.

Installing electrical outlets outdoors should be left to a licensed electrician, unless you are experienced in electrical installations and you follow the necessary safety precautions. Be sure to check your local electrical codes for requirements and permits before starting any electrical installation.

INDEX

U.S./Metric Measure Conversion Chart

	Formulas for Exact Measures				Rounded Measures for Quick Reference		
	Symbol	When you know:	Multiply by:	To find:			
Mass (weight)	oz	ounces	28.35	grams	1 oz		= 30 g
	lb	pounds	0.45	kilograms	4 oz		= 115 g
	g	grams	0.035	ounces	8 oz		= 225 g
	kg	kilograms	2.2	pounds	16 oz	= 1 lb	= 450 g
					32 oz	= 2 lb	= 900 g
					36 oz	= 2¼ lb	= 1000 g (1 kg)
Volume	pt	pints	0.47	liters	1 c	= 8 oz	= 250 ml
	qt	quarts	0.95	liters	2 c (1 pt)	= 16 oz	= 500 ml
	gal	gallons	3.785	liters	4 c (1 qt)	= 32 oz	= 1 liter
	ml	milliliters	0.034	fluid ounces	4 qt (1 gal)	= 128 oz	= 3¾ liter
Length	in.	inches	2.54	centimeters	⅜ in.	= 1.0 cm	
	ft	feet	30.48	centimeters	1 in.	= 2.5 cm	
	yd	yards	0.9144	meters	2 in.	= 5.0 cm	
	mi	miles	1.609	kilometers	2½ in.	= 6.5 cm	
	km	kilometers	0.621	miles	12 in. (1 ft)	= 30 cm	
	m	meters	1.094	yards	1 yd	= 90 cm	
	cm	centimeters	0.39	inches	100 ft	= 30 m	
					1 mi	= 1.6 km	
Temperature	° F	Fahrenheit	⅝ (after subtracting 32)	Celsius	32° F	= 0° C	
	° C	Celsius	⅞ (then add 32)	Fahrenheit	68° F	= 20° C	
					212° F	= 100° C	
Area	in.^{2}	square inches	6.452	square centimeters	1 in.^{2}	= 6.5 cm^2	
	ft^2	square feet	929.0	square centimeters	1 ft^2	= 930 cm^2	
	yd^2	square yards	8361.0	square centimeters	1 yd^2	= 8360 cm^2	
	a.	acres	0.4047	hectares	1 a.	= 4050 m^2	